FLIRTING OR HURTING?

A Teacher's Guide on Student-to-Student Sexual Harassment in Schools
(Grades 6 through 12)

Written by
Nan Stein and Lisa Sjostrom

A Joint Project of the
NEA Women and Girls Center for Change
and the Wellesley College Center for Research on Women

AN NEA PROFESSIONAL LIBRARY PUBLICATION
NATIONAL EDUCATION ASSOCIATION
Washington, DC

Note: The opinions expressed in this publication do not necessarily represent the policy or position of the National Education Association. Materials published by the NEA Professional Library are intended to be discussion documents for educators who are concerned with specialized interests of the profession.

Library of Congress Cataloging-in-Publication Data

Stein, Nan D., 1947–
    Flirting or hurting: a teacher's guide on student-to-student sexual harassment in schools (grades 6 through 12) / by Nan Stein and Lisa Sjostrom.
        p. cm.—
    "An NEA Professional Library publication."
    Includes bibliographical references.
    ISBN 0-8106-1864-8
    1. Sexual harassment in education—United States—Handbooks, manuals, etc. 2. Students—United States—Conduct of life—Handbooks, manuals, etc. I. Sjostrom, Lisa. II. Title. LC212.8.S74 1994
        370.19'345—dc20   94-32746
                                                                                        CIP

CONTENTS

Chapter 4. Supplemental Activities

Chapter 5. Resources

Appendix: Relevant Readings

No singular approach can eliminate and prevent sexual harassment in schools. This teacher's guide will better serve its purpose, and have both a longer lasting and a more profound effect, if you teach its lessons in a context where students are continually challenged to question broader social issues. For example, although this guide is not explicitly about either anti-Semitism or racism, do not hesitate to draw crucial links to those people who have taken or are taking a stand against injustice. Although this guide is not about popular culture, we encourage you to critique with your students the messages sent by the media, songs, movies, and videos. As discussion of sexual harassment widens to include broader questions of *why* and *how* human attitudes are shaped and behavior determined, we help students grasp the meaning of personal choice and social responsibility — not only to stand up to sexual harassment, but to social injustice as it appears in any guise: bullying, dating violence, racial and ethnic intolerance, gay bashing, hazing, and domestic violence/battering. Students need our encouragement to see themselves as makers of justice, transformers of injustice.

We must employ a multi-dimensional approach to combatting sexual harassment and introduce the following measures school-wide:

1. Age-appropriate, flexible materials. From the start, utilize the appropriate steps that your school or district has designated to introduce new teaching materials. The sexual harassment lessons could be offered in a variety of settings: in English, social studies, or health classes; through the guidance department via discussion groups; or through teacher/advisor sessions. To effectively pursue this topic, you must be prepared to do more than lead a discussion of the laws that cover sexual harassment in education and the workplace. Just reading students "the riot act" is not enough. Readings and writing assignments, as well as role plays and lively discussions, are essential.

2. Multiple training sessions. The full staff should attend training that provides, at a minimum, an overview of the problem of sexual harassment. Then, a core group of male and female teachers and administrators in every building who might serve as "ombudspeople" (we prefer this term to "complaint managers" or "sexual harassment grievance committee") should receive more intensive training. Training should include cafeteria workers, bus drivers, teacher's aides, janitors, adjunct music teachers, driver's education teachers, and coaches. This is important because schools are responsible for students' welfare not only during the school day, but also on the school bus and at any school-sponsored activity (a dance, sporting event, concert, field trip, etc.).

3. Appropriate in-school interventions. Your school may need to implement various interventions, such as:

- counseling for students who harass;
- counseling for students who are in abusive relationships;
- training peer leaders to conduct workshops for other students;
- peer mediation programs (with adult presence and participation).

4. Grievance policies and procedures. These should be accessible and readable, written in a language and parlance that students, staff, and parents can understand. The due process rights of the accused need to be protected; yet, your policies and procedures need to encourage students to come forward with complaints.

5. Parent and guardian involvement. When appropriate send a letter home to all parents prior to beginning this sexual harassment unit. Co-sign the letter with the principal. Be sure to indicate that the unit approaches the subject of sexual harassment as a civil rights issue, and not as a matter of sex education or values clarification. Also, consider holding a meeting for the parents to preview portions of the lessons.

Ultimately, a strategy to reduce and eliminate sexual harassment in schools needs to aim at a transformation of the broader school culture. Dealing effectively with sexual harassment is much easier if a school has committed itself to infusing a spirit of equity and including a critique of injustice in its curriculum and pedagogy. We need to view sexual harassment as a systemic problem and treat it with sustained and multi-dimensional educational efforts.

ACKNOWLEDGMENTS

This project has been a co-production from the beginning. Inspiration and support came from Pam Ryan, Claudia Edwards, and Roger Stephon of the NEA Women and Girls Center for Change, a unit of the National Education Association's Human and Civil Rights Division (HCR), and from the former director of HCR, Dr. Charles T. Williams. Nora Todd from the Massachusetts Teachers Association (MTA) helped recruit teachers to pilot these lessons; much credit is due her and the staff at the Professional Development Division of the MTA.

Forty-six classroom teachers taught, evaluated, and contributed revisions to the guide. They allowed us into their classrooms, formulated hard questions, offered pedagogical alternatives, and filled out countless evaluation forms. They also endured frequent memos and reminders from us, for which they got fed only once. They willingly posed for a group photograph so we could track them down should they fail to fill out all the evaluation forms. This guide is as much the teachers' as it is ours. The teachers are truly our partners and co-conspirators, and we are indebted to them.

Forty-two teachers from various Massachusetts school districts both taught and evaluated the teacher's guide (listed alphabetically by district): Herb Baker from Belmont; Kathryn Barr, John Nygren, and Pamela Turner from Beverly; Sue Curtin from Concord; Kathleen Dowling and Kathleen Dunn from Duxbury; Ellen Makynen and Nelma Wood from Framingham; Mardi Donovan, Joe Ferrari, and Barbara Ligon from Franklin; Karen Godfrey, Jean Jones, Elizabeth Moon, and Cathy Thibedeau from Hamilton-Wenham; Deborah Almy from Lincoln; Carmen Arnone, Suzanne Harrington, Bob Kain, and Marie Murray from Malden; Anne Caouette, Nancy Lane, and Gretchen Maurer from Mansfield; Gracie Burke and Rita Fontina from Milton; Jim Cieri and Peg Downing from Nashoba; Nancy Beardall, Nancy Cohen, Lisa Erdekian, Marj Montgomery, and Rosanne Perlmutter from Newton; Mary Mahoney and Eula Walsh from Sudbury; Carla Scuzzarella from Watertown; Marcia Goldsmith, Kelli Trudel, and James Stone from Wayland; Judith Ferrari from Westboro; and Chris Dion and Ellie Malick from Weymouth. Four other teachers used the guide in their classrooms: Jane Vodoklys from Framingham; Harold Williams from Franklin; Sue Lancella from Hamilton-Wenham; and Joyce Calligan from Nashoba.

Additional revisions were suggested by Bill Bigelow, author and high school teacher in Portland, Oregon; and by Eleanor Linn, Associate Director of the Programs for Educational Opportunity at the School of Education, University of Michigan. As always, they came through with provocative critiques and questions that sent us back to the drawing board or, as the case may be, the computer screen.

The title of this guide was suggested by Scott Ondovchik, a student in Deborah Almy's seventh grade social studies class at the Hanscom Air Force Base Middle School in Lincoln. Deborah describes Scott as a quiet boy who is very proud that he is sensitive to other people's troubles. Scott is in the boys' choir and on the wrestling team.

Our final thanks go to Scott and the hundreds of other Massachusetts public school students who participated in the development of this teacher's guide.

NAN STEIN
LISA SJOSTROM

CHAPTER 1. INTRODUCTION

Don't Skip This Section

Preparation

If necessary, before you begin, utilize the appropriate steps that your school district has designated to introduce new teaching materials in a school. Then, read through the entire guide and tailor a program to suit the particular time restrictions, age group, and other related lessons of your classroom. See the Table of Contents for a quick overview of the lessons and "Suggested Teaching Format" in Chapter 2 for a description of options. You may want to cull words from the lessons onto a vocabulary list for your students to define and refer to throughout the unit, as well as prepare folders and/or journals in which students can collect handouts and record thoughts.

Flexibility and Options

This guide may be used effectively in a variety of courses in grades 6 through 12. The lessons follow in a purposeful sequential order based on the collective thinking of approximately 50 teachers who piloted the guide in their classrooms. All of the "Core Lessons" (Chapter 3) should be included in the unit and, though most effectively taught over consecutive days, the lessons may be spread out over a number of weeks. Freely include additional exercises from the "Supplemental Activities" (Chapter 4) as your time and interest allow.

Some Opening Notes on Teaching Style

The issue of sexual harassment is emotionally charged and personal in nature. You need to create as safe a space as possible for students to honestly discuss their experiences, opinions, and feelings. The following points are suggested as ways to help create a safe environment.

Respect. Teachers and facilitators need to model respectful behavior. It is crucial to take seriously and be sensitive to students' individual differences and perspectives, as well as any discomfort students may experience in discussing an emotional, personal, and perhaps scary topic. If students become defensive, start acting out, or giggling, take time to talk with them about what they find difficult.

Judgment. Be careful not to make judgments or incriminations. Don't reinforce the stereotypes, for example, that "boys will be boys" or that girls are powerless "victims." Keep the focus on the facts.

Disclosure. You should think through beforehand strategies for dealing with any cases of sexual harassment and abuse that may be evoked by these lessons or disclosed during discussions. Sometimes all a student needs is someone who will listen. Sometimes, you may need to refer students to the school psychologist or counselor.

If a student recounts an incident of physical sexual harassment between an adult staff member and a student, be sure to follow the procedures required in your state law and school district policy.

Safety and Ground Rules. Ask the students themselves what they need from you and from each other in order to feel safe talking about sexual harassment. For example, do they require confidentiality, or do they need the right to refuse to participate? To foster open discussion, lay down ground rules before you begin each exercise. For example, before a discussion students can be reminded: that everyone's input matters; to listen to one another without interrupting; and to talk about people and situations they know, but without mentioning specific names.

If discussion becomes heated, remind students that there are ways to disagree respectfully without resorting to name calling or insults. To refocus the class, you can ask students to put their thoughts in writing (see "A Selection of Writing Options" in Chapter 2).

Another way to create safety for students is to set up a "question box" in which students can anonymously pose questions that might be difficult to raise in front of peers. You then can read aloud and answer questions in class without reference to individuals.

Diversity. When dividing students for group exercises, aim to create groups that mix the students by sex, race, and ethnic background. Students may initially feel more comfortable or express that they want to be in sex segregated groups, but one of the goals of this project is to open communication across gender, racial, and ethnic lines.

Language. The language you establish for class discussions will help determine the attitudes students take away from the unit. In particular, avoid using the word "victim" when describing the "target" of sexual harassment. Targets are not powerless. This guide provides numerous examples of actions both targets and bystanders can take in response to sexual harassment incidents.

Use both the pronouns "he" and "she" when referring to targets of sexual harassment. Sexual harassment is not only a "girls' issue" in school or a "women's issue" in society. Sexual harassment affects both girls and boys in school, and both women and men in the workplace. Preventing sexual harassment is everyone's responsibility.

Some 6th and 7th grade students, just beginning to date and flirt, may not initially identify with the term "sexual harassment." However, these younger students readily relate to experiences where "teasing" may have crossed the line into "bullying." Using the term "bullying" or "sexual bullying" may make sexual harassment easier to understand for younger students.

If you see what you consider to be an incident of student-to-student sexual harassment in school, one of the most effective ways to stop the behavior is to say: "This is inappropriate behavior for school. That's not allowed here." It is not wise to label the behavior "sexual harassment" because, given the subjective definition of sexual harassment, students might respond to you by saying, "We both like this, it's mutual." For similar reasons, avoid the response: "That offends me!"

Use in Various Classrooms and *Always* in Coed Settings

Sexual harassment is a relevant topic in many courses. Exactly where it is appropriate to use the materials will differ in each school. Where possible, you may find it helpful to co-teach the lessons. A male/female team, in particular, sends a powerful message to students about the relevance of sexual harassment to both sexes. This is critical: You should not make male students feel threatened by the topic.

History, Social Studies and Contemporary Issues Classes. Sexual harassment is not a new phenomenon — it is deeply rooted in our culture and our history. You can expand upon these lessons to include an historic review of discrimination against women and other disenfranchised groups, including discussion of slavery, women's suffrage, or the labor movement. Alternatively, this guide also can help you incorporate its lessons into classes about broad movements for social change, such as the civil rights movement and the women's movement. Likewise, broader discussions of Title IX and other federal and state anti-discrimination laws that have been passed to redress past inequities and provide equal protection in housing, public accommodation, jobs, and education could easily include a unit on sexual harassment. Several exercises are suitable for use during Women's History Month.

English Classes. Many activities contain writing components or are followed by homework writing assignments. Chapter 2 also provides a section of writing options that may be used at your discretion at any point as you progress through the guide. Students can keep an eye out for incidents of sex bias, discrimination and sexual harassment in the novels and stories they read. Many novels, short stories, poems, plays, folktales, and myths are suitable to use in conjunction with this guide. Possible starting points include *I Know Why the Caged Bird Sings* by Maya Angelou; *Villette* by Charlotte Bronte; *The Color Purple* by Alice Walker; *The Bell Jar* by Sylvia Plath; *The Taming of the Shrew* by William Shakespeare; the poems "A Just

Anger" and "Unlearning to Not Speak" by Marge Piercy in *Circles on the Water, Selected Poems of Marge Piercy* (1982); and the poem "A Song of Sojourner Truth" by June Jordan in *Naming Our Destiny, New and Selected Poems* (1989).

Health and Physical Education Classes. Issues of sexual harassment and bullying can be incorporated into discussions about "Getting Along," "Dating," or "Respect." Since sexual harassment is part of the continuum of violence in interpersonal relationships, discussion may be expanded to include issues of teen and dating violence, as well as battering and domestic violence.

Guidance Discussion Groups. This guide can be used in conjunction with broader discussions about social norms, respect, decision making, gender bias, conflict resolution, dating, teen violence, interpersonal relations, power dynamics, or career education. The materials in this guide are also suitable for use in support groups for students enrolled in non-traditional classes in vocational/technical high schools.

CHAPTER 2. OTHER PRELIMINARY NOTES

A Selection of Writing Options

Class and homework writing assignments have been built directly into many of the exercises in this guide. We also invite you to weave spontaneous journal and "freewriting" assignments into classes at various points. The following options are particularly effective when class discussion and dynamics become heated, complicated, or difficult; or when particular students become defensive or overbearing. At such moments, student writing may serve to "democratize" the class discussion. Putting a pen to paper often gives students the chance to regain composure, collect thoughts, and safely express feelings and opinions that might get lost in the larger or louder discussion. You then can return to discussion or begin the next class by asking for student volunteers to read their writing aloud.

Freewrites in the Midst of Class Discussions. At any point during discussion, ask students to write a response to one of the following questions:

- What would you like to add to this conversation right now?

- What do you think of "Sam's" point? Write him a short letter of explanation.

- Do you agree or disagree with what "Anna" just said? Why?

Homework Writing Assignments after Class Discussions. Choose from the following options and ask students to write a specified number of pages at home:

- Summarize the various viewpoints expressed in the discussion.

- Express and defend your own opinion.

- Choose one argument/statement made in class with which you strongly agree/disagree, and explain why.

- Choose one thing said in class that bothered or outraged you and "talk back."

- Continue this discussion in a written dialogue. (Ask students to assign fictitious names to people involved in the written conversation.)

Freewrites After Case Studies, Role Plays, or a Review of a Sexual Harassment Incident. After concluding discussion of a case or incident, ask students to write one of the following options:

- Write a diary entry or interior monologue in the voice of the target, bystander, or harasser: "Put yourself in his/her shoes and tell what's happening, what you are thinking, and how you feel at this moment." (Assign portions of the class different roles to explore.)

- Same as above with an added stipulation: each piece should end with the statement, "I don't know what to do." (Ask students to read these pieces aloud and have the class brainstorm responses in a discussion; or, ask students to swap papers with a neighbor and respond in writing on the same page. Ask for volunteers to read their questions and responses to the class.)

- Add *yourself* to the scene as a third party bystander: "If you *saw* this happening, what would you do?" (Ask students to write their own conclusions to the scene with themselves playing critical roles.)

- Assume the role of an older/younger sibling of the character in the case who is being sexually harassed and write down a dinner table conversation that involves discussion of the incident.

- Write a hypothetical dialogue between two people (already in the scene or whom you create), for example:

  1. A conversation about the incident between two bystanders.

  2. A conversation between a parent and child who is a target of harassment.

  3. An interchange/conversation between the target and the harasser.

  4. An interchange/conversation between a bystander and the harasser.

- Write a "dialogue poem" from the paired perspectives of two people involved in the situation. The poem consists of a number of two-line stanzas; the first line is written from one person's point of view, the second from another's. For example, you might compare the thoughts of a perpetrator and a target:

  > Time to go to school.
  > *Can't I stay home, ma — my stomach hurts.*
  >
  > Bus is late again!
  > *I hope the driver got lost.*
  >
  > She looks hot.
  > *Freeze, freeze him out.*
  >
  > Walk by me, baby.
  > *Quick, Bebe, make room on your seat...*

Freewrites or Homework in Response to a Comment, Quotation, Question, or Fact. Any provocative word or line from a case study, article, or discussion can be a springboard or "prompt" into writing. Write the prompt on the board and ask students to try one of the following options:

- Use the prompt as the starting point of a poem.
- Expand upon the prompt in your own words.
- Write a letter in which you expand upon or agree/disagree with the prompt.
- Write a short story in which the prompt appears at any point.

Examples of possible writing prompts (drawn from quotations in magazine articles):

- "Boys will be boys."
- "You feel like you're a car," said a 17-year-old girl. "It's like we're all cars in a car show."
- "Can't you take a joke?"
- "What part of 'NO' don't you understand?!"

Suggested Teaching Format

All of the "Core Lessons" (Chapter 3) should be included in the unit, along with any "Supplemental Activities" (Chapter 4) your time allows. Freely tailor lessons to suit your own classroom and time frame. For example, you may want to augment a case study with a writing exercise, devote extra time to a particular discussion, or create a homework assignment of your own.

Core Lessons

Class 1

Flirting vs. Sexual Harassment ◆ a teacher-led discussion

> *Homework:* "Crossing the Line" student writing

> *Objectives:* To raise student awareness about the kinds of sexual harassment which take place all the time; to discern the fluid, subjective line between flirting and harassment; to encourage open student discussion of a complicated topic.

Long-term assignment

Taking A Closer Look ◆ student observations and note-taking

> *Objectives:* To encourage students to be "anthropologists" and "ethnographers" in their own school; to recognize sexual harassment.

Class 2

Says Who? ◆ a questionnaire and debriefing

> *Objectives:* To define sexual harassment; to dispel common myths about sexual harassment; to raise awareness of the prevalence of sexual harassment; to inform students of their legal rights in school.

Class 3

What are Your Rights? ◆ a review and discussion

> *Objectives:* To define sexual harassment; to inform students of their legal rights; to review school policy and procedures on sexual harassment; to review possible ways for targets of sexual harassment to respond.

Classes 4 and 5

Case Studies and Role Plays ♦ class review and case presentations

Class 4: Class review of a case; student team preparation of second cases

Class 5: Case presentations and role-plays; teacher debriefing

> *Objectives:* To grapple with the complicated factors involved in occurrences of sexual harassment; to try on the roles and respond from the perspectives of various people involved in actual cases of sexual harassment; to determine responsibility in these cases.

Class 6

Get Up, Stand Up for Your Rights ♦ a brainstorm and action planning

> *Homework:* "Taking a Stand," a personal essay

> *Objectives:* To discuss strategies to eliminate sexual harassment; to explore what it means to be a justice-maker; to remind students that they have had the experience of proactively responding when a situation needed righting.

Supplemental Activities

One class period

Send a Letter to the Harasser ♦ a review and in-class writing assignment

> *Objectives:* To inform students about a possible way to respond if they are targets of student-to-student sexual harassment.

One-half class period

In the News ♦ a review of seventeen press conference statements about sexual harassment

> *Homework:* "In the News," article writing assignment

> *Objectives:* To understand the value of speaking out publicly about sexual harassment.

Once a month

Current Events ♦ a monthly discussion

> *Objectives:* To raise student awareness of current issues concerning sexual harassment in the news; to ensure ongoing discussion.

Over the course of a week

Straight from the Source ♦ an interview with a respected adult about sex roles and sexual harassment

> *In-Class Writing:* "An Accordion Poem," a group assignment

> *Objectives:* To connect with an adult and hear firsthand about growing up as a man or a woman; to ask questions and draw one's own conclusions; to learn from another's personal experience.

One class period

Cartoons ♦ an art activity

> *Objectives:* To encourage creative, proactive responses to sexual harassment by third party bystanders.

One class period

Respect ♦ a brainstorm and discussion

> *Homework:* "Letter to a Young Friend," writing assignment

> *Objectives:* To allow students to define for themselves how they'd like to be treated by others in social situations and in general. To reinforce that we can determine our own behavior toward others and insist upon respectful treatment for ourselves.

Topical Cross-Reference of Activities

General Topic	Activity
Perception of Social Norms	Flirting vs. Sexual Harassment; Taking a Closer Look; Says Who?; Straight from the Source; Respect
Perception of Sexual Harassment	Flirting vs. Sexual Harassment; Taking a Closer Look; Current Events; Straight from the Source; In the News
Myths about Sexual Harassment	Taking a Closer Look; Says Who?; Respect
Definition of Sexual Harassment	Flirting vs. Sexual Harassment; Crossing the Line; Says Who?; What are Your Rights?; Case Studies; In the News; Current Events
Information about Legal Rights	Says Who?; What Are Your Rights?; Case Studies; Get Up, Stand Up for Your Rights
Strategies to Prevent Sexual Harassment	Says Who?; What are Your Rights?; Case Studies; Get Up, Stand Up For Your Rights; In the News
Responses to Harassment: Target	Crossing the Line; What Are Your Rights?; Case Studies; Get Up, Stand Up for Your Rights; Send a Letter to the Harasser (Another Student); In the News
Responses to Harassment: Bystanders	Taking a Closer Look; Case Studies; Get Up, Stand Up for Your Rights; Cartoons

CHAPTER 3. CORE LESSONS

Lesson 1. Flirting vs. Sexual Harassment:

A Teacher-led Discussion

Objectives

To raise student awareness about the kinds of sexual harassment which take place all the time; to discern the fluid, subjective line between flirting and sexual harassment; to encourage open student discussion of a complicated topic.

Preparation

☑ Prepare three lists with headings and subheadings either on the blackboard or on big sheets of newsprint (these sheets may be used as reference points in later lessons). The titles of the three lists should read "Verbal or Written," "Gestures," and "Physical." Under each heading, write the two subheadings "Flirting" and "Harassment." During the discussion, anticipate creating a third subheading on each of the three lists titled "Depends." At this point, the three lists should look like this:

Verbal or Written		**Gestures**		**Physical**	
Flirting	Harassment	Flirting	Harassment	Flirting	Harassment

☑ Decide beforehand if you will allow students to use profanity or if they should speak in euphemisms. Another alternative is for students to write their answers on paper and hand these to you to decide what to record on the lists.

 Ask students to arrange their chairs in a circle, if possible.

 Decide upon the ground rules, e.g.:

1) Everyone must listen when someone is speaking.

2) Don't get personal by mentioning anyone's name when telling about a specific incident.

3) Ask students to determine other rules, such as "What's said here, stays here."

Encourage younger students, in particular, to be in their most "mature" behavior mode.

Introduction

"This activity is pretty simple and fun. We're going to talk about the difference between flirting and sexual harassment. Before we begin, I want to state from the outset that we're not here to demonize or blame boys. Many of us may never be either targets of sexual harassment or perpetrators. But all of us are *witnesses and bystanders* who may see sexual harassment happening, and we need to learn to say, 'Hey, cut it out, that's not funny!,' or 'What would you do if this were your sister, your mom, or your brother?' So, we're not just trying to change boys and men. We're trying to change *all* of us — so we'll have the courage to actively respond when we see sexual harassment going on.

"You are the best anthropologists of your own culture — and 'subcultures' (cliques, who you 'hang' with). All the time, you are observing other kids' behaviors in school, and you see how behaviors differ depending on where you are and whether there are adults around or not — in classrooms, locker rooms, the cafeteria, the parking lot, the hallways. In this discussion, I want you to draw upon what *you* already know and see. You are the experts and sophisticated 'critiquers' of your subcultures.

"In this exercise, we're going to talk about how you interact with each other and what you observe, how you make sense between what is sexual harassment and what is flirting ('hanging out,' 'getting to know someone').

"First we'll focus on verbal or written exchanges, such as comments and notes. Then we'll focus on gestures like winking, waving and other ways you communicate without speaking or touching. Lastly we'll consider physical interactions. For each category, we'll talk about examples of flirting and then instances that cross the line into sexual harassment. I don't expect everyone to agree. What's most important is that we start talking. Can anyone give me an example of a comment or a note that's flirtatious and nice...?"

Activity

 To avoid confusion, walk students through the lists one at a time.

 Write down student answers under the appropriate subheading.

 Encourage students to stay with specifics they know from a school setting and not stray to hypothetical or out-of-school situations.

 If one column isn't being addressed, ask students specific questions; e.g.: "Can you give me examples of physical ways people flirt?"

 When students disagree upon the nature of a particular behavior or comment, ask them what criteria they are basing their opinion upon and enter this under a heading "Depends." For example, perhaps the nature of a comment *depends* upon whether the speaker is a friend or a stranger, or upon their tone of voice. Write these dependent variables on the appropriate list.

If one behavior falls under both headings of "Flirting" and "Harassment," note this by drawing an arrow from one column to the other, e.g.:

Verbal or Written		Gestures		Physical	
Flirting	Harassment	Flirting	Harassment	Flirting	Harassment
You look nice →		blowing kiss →		hug	pinch
Like your hair	Nice ass	wink	grab own crotch	hold hands	grabbing
	'ho	wave	lip licking		

depends

tone of voice
how they look at you
who else is around

depends

friend or stranger
how old they are
in public or in private

depends

friend or stranger
where you are

Questions to Raise Afterwards

After students have completed the activity, the following discussion questions can help them make sense of the lists:

1. Why do people define sexual harassment differently?

2. If sexual harassment is illegal in schools, how come it goes on?

3. Who allows sexual harassment to go on?

4. What are some common forms of sexual harassment that often go unnoticed in schools?

5. Do girls sexually harass other girls?

6. Who harasses boys?

Troubleshooting

Discussion often gets heated and students can raise many challenging questions. Here are some typical questions and scenarios, along with suggested responses:

1) Students interrupt one another, everyone begins talking and disagreeing at once.

    "We all have to be in the same conversation, so we all have to listen. We don't need to achieve consensus. It's good to travel through lots of opinions and disagreements because this is a complicated subject for everyone. Every definition of sexual harassment contains a subjective component, meaning the target can define the harassment. So, if you're confused, that's to be expected."

2) Boys raise the argument that girls are asking to be harassed by the way they dress.

    "All of our opinions about temptation are shaped by the times we live in. Did you know that in Puritanical New England in the 1600's if a woman wore a dress and her ankles or wrists showed, men would walk on the other side of the street and turn their eyes away in horror? They believed that the Devil was tempting them!

    "Sometimes we — both males and females — do dress to look good and feel good about ourselves. Yes, we may want attention, but that doesn't mean we want to be harassed. There are different types of attention, as we're noting on these lists."

3) Students ask: "But how do you know which is which? We won't be able to say anything to one another!"

"We're figuring this out all the time — silently. You don't ever go up to someone and say, 'Hi, can we flirt now?' This is why we need to keep talking and openly discussing our intentions, feelings, and interpretations of each other's words and behaviors."

4) Students ask about other hassles that don't fall under the category of sexual harassment.

Crank calls: "Against the law. It is a crime under both state and federal laws for anyone to make obscene or harassing phone calls. Look in the front section of the telephone book — it's spelled out there, and tells you to call the phone company if these calls persist."

Knocking books out of someone's hands: "Someone's provoking you, but this isn't sexual in nature, so isn't covered by federal law. Of course, the school may have its own rules about student behavior, such as rules against cheating and fighting. And remember, something doesn't have to be illegal for you to say, 'This is making me uncomfortable!' or 'You're acting like a jerk!'"

Being harassed by a family member at home: "Federal laws on sex discrimination and sexual harassment only apply to two places: one law covers school and school-sponsored events, and a second law covers the workplace. Of course, sexual assault at home or on the streets is just as serious. So speak up, say 'no,' tell someone you trust and keep telling until you find someone who believes you and will help you."

5) "Can a harasser get sued?"

"Yes and No. Under the federal law called Title IX, "you bring a complaint against the school district and ask for monetary damages. Why? Because it's the school district's responsibility to enforce the rules and explain what's legal and illegal in school. Under law, the school district has to provide you with an environment that is safe and equal for learning for both girls and boys. So, the school district is responsible for maintaining a school climate and environment that is conducive to learning and one that allows everyone to participate without fear of sexual harassment. Though an individual cannot get sued under Title IX, if the person has done something that is also criminal (like assault), then the district attorney may choose to sue the individual in criminal court."

6) A student relates an incident of teen-dating violence that occurred away from the school.

"Violence is a separate category from sexual harassment. Violence in teen relationships or domestic violence is a form of *assault* and is covered by criminal law. For that, you need to make a complaint through the police and the district attorney."

7) Students feel uncomfortable due to some of the language and examples used in the discussion.

"Yes, this *should* make you feel uncomfortable — because that's what sexual harassment does."

8) A student asks, "If sexual harassment is illegal, then why has it gone on for so long?"

"Laws were passed regarding sex discrimination in 1972, and sexual harassment is a form of sex discrimination. Schools didn't get the message that they are responsible and can be sued for monetary damages until a Supreme Court ruling in 1992. Just as with the history of the fight for civil rights in our country, it often takes time for laws to translate into changes in people's and institutions' behaviors."

9) A student discloses sexual contact with a teacher.

After class, to the student: "You need to speak with Title IX officer [the counselor, the principal]. I will take you to the appropriate place so you can report this behavior."

10) A student asks, "What makes harassment 'sexual'? What's the difference between harassment and sexual harassment?"

"Sexual harassment happens because of your particular sex: because you are a girl or because you are a boy. Sexual harassment applies to a certain gender. For example, boys can be teased about certain body parts and girls can be teased about others. Such behavior is inappropriate behavior for school and violates your privacy. Additionally bumping into another person is not the equivalent to grabbing a private area of your body."

11) A student asks, "What if someone's falsely accused?"

All allegations of sexual harassment are very serious; people's lives and reputations can be damaged. If it is found that a student has made a false accusation, the school administration has to think about a policy to address these situations.

Objectives

To discern the line between flirting and harassment, as well as the intentions and feelings of people involved. To introduce the responsibility of third party bystanders.

Assignment

Ask students to write a short story about a time when flirting between students crosses the line into sexual harassment. Instruct them to try to base their story on an incident they have seen at school, using false names, and *not* to resolve the conflict in their stories (students will be asked to generate responses in the debriefing). Additional instructions:

 Feel free to draw upon the lists created in the "Flirting vs. Harassment" activity.

 Characters can be any age and either gender.

 Include descriptions: where and when the situation is happening, characters' names, their appearance, and so on.

 Include characters' dialogue, thoughts, and feelings.

 Since both flirting and sexual harassment usually happen in public, include other people who see what is happening.

 End the story with the target of harassment saying, "I don't know what to do" or posing the question, "What should I do?"

Debriefing

After students have handed in and you have reviewed their stories, choose several stories to read aloud to the class. Ask students if they'd prefer you to read the writings without identifying the authors or if they'd feel more comfortable reading their own. Possible discussion questions for the class:

1. Is this flirting or sexual harassment? How can you tell?

2. What should the target do now? (If students are stumped,

lay out options to choose from, e.g., ignore him/her? say
something? tell a friend?)

3. If you were standing nearby and saw this happen, what
   would you do?

☑ During this discussion it can be very powerful to ask students to improvise
on the spur-of-the-moment as either targets or bystanders; students then
get the chance to "try on," and see one another taking, proactive stances. For
example, during discussion of a story where a girl is harassed by a boy, the teacher
spontaneously asks a student named "Louisa" the following questions:

> "What would you say in this situation, 'Louisa'? *If* 'Serge' (sitting
> behind her) were harassing you, what could you say to get him
> to stop? Turn around and respond…"

Lesson 2:
Taking a
Closer Look

Student Observations

(over several
days or a week)

Objectives

To encourage students to be "anthropologists" and "ethnographers" in their
school; to recognize sexual harassment.

Background Note

Ethnography is a type of qualitative research that attempts to describe a culture or
aspects of a culture. Sometimes referred to as "thick description," ethnography is a
sister science of anthropology. Ethnographic research is rich in description of people, places, and conversations. Data are collected in the field, in the setting where
subjects normally spend their time, as opposed to laboratories or other
researcher-controlled sites. An ethnographer begins a study as a cultural "out-
sider" and attempts to view the culture from the frame of reference of the people
studied. Through the keeping of a detailed record of what she/he hears and
observes, an ethnographer eventually begins to possess an "insider's" view.
Ethnographers are interested not only in people's behavior, but also in the shared
meanings people attribute to events within a culture (e.g., the various meanings of
a wink, or the raising of hands in a classroom).*

Preparation

 Photocopy and distribute the following
handout "Take a Closer Look."

Ⓥ If students will record notes on index cards
or in "blue books," distribute these to the class.

Introduction

Ⓥ Ask students to name areas in the school known to 'belong' to certain
groups, for example, the area outside the boys' or girls' bathrooms, a certain section of the lunchroom, the gym, the playground, the parking lot, certain
stairwells, etc. Compile a list on the board.

 "You know more about the subcultures (cliques, who 'hangs' with whom) in
this school than anyone else. You are the experts and sophisticated 'critiquers'
of what goes on here. You observe students' and teachers' behaviors day in and day
out. You know what really goes on and how students' words and actions differ
depending on where they are and whether there are adults around or not. So,
you're in a great position to be ethnographers."

---

*   *The "Background Note" on ethnography is taken from Qualitative Research for Education, by Robert C.
    Bogden and Sari Knopp Biklen (Allyn and Bacon, Needham Heights, MA, 1982).*

Assignment

✔ Read the handout "Take a Closer Look…" aloud with students and explain that over the next few days (or weeks) they are to assume the role of ethnographers and observe the way students treat each other in school. They should focus on students' language, gestures, and physical actions. Ask the class to take special note of times where behavior or language "crosses the line" from teasing into bullying or from flirting into sexual harassment:

1. Ask or assign students (or student teams) to 'cover' one specific place or hangout over the next few days or, on their own, students can cover the whole school.

2. Ask students to jot down their observational notes as inconspicuously as possible in a specific notebook, journal, or on index cards, without identifying people by name.

3. Ask students to observe the behavior of younger children in school as well as their peers.

✔ Assure students that the point of this activity is not to "snitch," "rat," "tattle," or inform on one another. Rather, they are taking on the role of ethnographers to gather information that can be used to raise awareness of the subcultures in which they are all participating or observing daily.

✔ Encourage students to see themselves as activists as well as ethnographers. Tell students that noting injustices is crucial, but only a first step. Injustices call out to be righted — through action. The action activity "Get Up, Stand Up for Your Rights" (see Lesson 6) is the linchpin of these core lessons. Inform students before they begin this exercise that after taking a closer look they will review and begin taking necessary actions to make the school a more just and democratic place.

Debriefing

✔ You may set aside one specific time to discuss students' observations, or ask students to "check in" during several minutes at the start or the end of each class. Students may be surprised to realize how often, and on what a continual basis, "lines get crossed."

✔ Ask students to report on their observations, without identifying names, in either a teacher-led discussion or with one another in small groups (in which case, discussion questions may be written on the board or handed out for the students to ask one another).

Students may uncover injustices and incidents of sexual harassment as they discuss their observations. This is a time to encourage students to take actions to remedy such situations (see the "Get Up, Stand Up for Your Rights" activity, Lesson 6).

To help students make sense of their observations, follow with a general class discussion:

1. Where and when does sexual harassment happen?
2. Who gets sexually harassed in school?
3. Was race or social class a factor?
4. Did anyone try to stop it? What happened, or why not?
5. What is being "said," in a sense, when someone doesn't speak up and intervene?
6. How did you feel as a bystander?
7. What did you do in response, or what could you do if you saw this again next week?
8. Do these incidents follow any patterns?

Optional Activity

Ask students to draw a symbolic picture of what sexual harassment feels or looks like. You may give students the option of drawing with their "wrong" hand in order to relieve the pressure to make a "accurate" representation.

TAKE A CLOSER LOOK
BE AN ETHNOGRAPHER IN SCHOOL

An ethnographer is a specific kind of anthropologist, not unlike an objective reporter, who watches and writes down what happens in a particular culture or place. Some ethnographers travel the world to document how people live and behave in Eskimo villages or the Sahara Desert, but it isn't necessary to go that far away to take a closer look.

An ethnographer also can study and describe the culture of a living room, an amusement park, or any city block. All that's needed to be an ethnographer is an open pair of eyes and ears, and a good set of questions. These questions help you see things that have been in front of you all along, but which you might not have really noticed before.

Take a closer look at the way students treat one another in school: in your classes, in the hallways, during lunch period, in the locker rooms, and on the bus. What do you see? What do you hear? Before you start taking notes, read the following tips and starting questions. Then add questions of your own on the back of the page.

Ethnography Tips

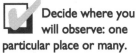 Decide where you will observe: one particular place or many.

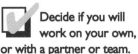 Decide if you will work on your own, or with a partner or team.

 Watch for instances where words, gestures, or actions cross the line from teasing into bullying or from flirting into sexual harassment.

 Write your ethnography notes in a special notebook, blue book, or on index cards.

 Jot down observations as inconspicuously as possible.

 Write down the setting (day, time, place), as well as the behavior you see, what you hear, who is involved, and the reactions of anyone else nearby.

 Don't mention names. Instead, refer to people generally, such as "a 10th grade girl," or "a middle school boy."

 Take note of both younger and older students in school.

Some Starting Questions

ᕗ Which areas of the school seem to "belong" to certain groups of students?

ᕗ What goes on between students that makes you uncomfortable or angry?

ᕗ When boys are together and a girl walks by, what happens? How do girls respond?

ᕗ Where, when, and how do words and actions cross the line from teasing into bullying, or from flirting into sexual harassment? How can you tell a line is being crossed?

ᕗ How do boys talk about girls when they are just with other boys?

ᕗ Who gets harassed?

ᕗ How does race, social class, or popularity figure into sexual harassment?

ᕗ How do people respond when a line is crossed?

ᕗ When girls are together and a boy walks by, what happens? How do boys respond?

ᕗ How do girls talk about boys when they are just with other girls?

ᕗ What kinds of statements and drawings are written on desks and bathroom walls?

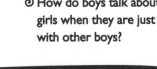

Lesson 3.
Says Who?

A Questionnaire and Debriefing

(one class period)

Objectives

To define sexual harassment; to dispel common myths about sexual harassment; to raise awareness of the prevalence of sexual harassment; to inform students of their legal rights in school.

Preparation

Review the "Says Who?" questionnaire (p. 26) and the "Teacher Answer Guide" (pp. 27-34). Photocopy the questionnaire for each student.

Activity

 Hand out the questionnaire and ask students individually to indicate whether they "Agree" or "Disagree" with each statement. If students disagree or are undecided, ask them to write down the reason why or what further information they need to decide. (They can write on the back of the handout.)

After students complete the questionnaire, ask them to gather in groups of three or four to decide upon and discuss three of the statements:

> "Choose and discuss the three most debatable, controversial questions, that is to say: the statements you had the hardest time responding to. Choose a 'recorder' and a 'reporter' for your group. The reporter should take notes on the main points of your discussion (you don't all have to come to agreement). The reporter will present the main points to the class."

 While students discuss and debate, visit each group and take note of which statements are the hottest topics of discussion.

Debriefing

Review the statements students have highlighted in their discussions, with group 'reporters' giving initial feedback to the class. After students have explored their own thoughts, offer more insight and information from the provided "Teacher Answer Guide." Statistics can be written on the board for students to see and analyze. Note: The answer guide for teachers supplies important background information. Be careful not to bog down the student discussion with too much information.

Since some of the questions do not have strictly right or wrong answers, encourage students to explain the reasoning for their chosen answer, as well as to indicate what further information they need to arrive at an informed opinion. It is important to help students think through how information shapes their opinions — or does not change their beliefs a bit.

Optional Activity

To open up a cross-generational conversation, ask students to take the questionnaire home and share it with members of their parents' and grandparents' generations.

SAYS WHO?
A QUESTIONNAIRE

☑ Read each statement.

☑ Check "A" if you agree with the statement.

☑ Check "D" if you disagree with the statement.

A D

☐ ☐ 1. Sexual harassment is just having fun.

☐ ☐ 2. If I'm being sexually harassed by an adult in school, there's nothing I can do.

☐ ☐ 3. If no one else sees me being harassed, there's nothing I can do because the harasser will just say I'm lying.

☐ ☐ 4. If I've flirted with this person in the past, then I asked to be sexually harassed.

☐ ☐ 5. Girls cannot sexually harass other girls.

☐ ☐ 6. Boys cannot be sexually harassed by girls.

☐ ☐ 7. If a girl wears a short skirt or tight jeans, she is asking to be sexually harassed.

A D

☐ ☐ 8. Girls' bodies are the only thing that matters to most boys.

☐ ☐ 9. A boy who claims he has been sexually harassed is a nerd, wimp, sissy, or "wuss."

☐ ☐ 10. Writing dirty things about someone on a bathroom wall at school is sexual harassment.

A D

☐ ☐ 11. If sexual harassment happens in your school, the school district can be sued in court.

☐ ☐ 12. When a girl says "no," she really means "yes" or "maybe" or "later."

☐ ☐ 13. If a girl says she is being sexually harassed and the boy says he is only fooling, then it's not sexual harassment.

☐ ☐ 14. Sexual harassment isn't a serious problem in school since it only affects a few people.

☐ ☐ 15. If you ignore sexual harassment, more than likely it will stop.

☐ ☐ 16. Boys are sexually harassed just as often as girls.

Teacher Answer Guide

Says Who? Questionnaire

1. **Sexual harassment is just having fun.**

   - Unlike flirting or good-natured joking, which are mutual interactions between two people, sexual harassment is unwelcomed and unwanted behavior which may cause the target to feel threatened, afraid, humiliated, angry, and often trapped.

   - If sexual harassment feels like fun to someone, it could be one-sided fun at someone else's expense.

   - Sexual harassment is about force, intimidation, power, and the disruption of the educational environment.

   - Sexual harassment is illegal and a violation of students' rights to receive equal educational opportunities.

2. **If I'm being sexually harassed by an adult in school, there's nothing I can do.**

   - If a person feels there is nothing they can do, it is because they are frightened or intimidated; or they have been lied to or threatened. They also may not know their rights.

   - Sexual harassment is serious and illegal.

   - If the sexual harassment between an adult in the school community and a minor (meaning a student) involves physical contact of a sexual nature, that adult may be committing child sexual abuse or assault, potentially criminal acts.

   - It is very important for a student to speak to a trusted adult about the alleged behavior. It might be very scary to point the finger at a particular adult — that adult may have power over a student's grade or be the person who would write them a letter of recommendation to college, for a job, or for a particular scholarship. That adult may be a popular person in the community, someone who brings pride and attention to the school. None of these are reasons enough to endure sexual attention or contact from an adult.

   - Please speak up for your own sake and for the sake of other students who over the years may have put up with these behaviors!

- Note: Ways to respond to sexual harassment are reviewed on the student handout "What Can I Do?," included in the "What are Your Rights" (Lesson 4); and on a second handout "Get Up, Stand Up for Your Rights," included in the "Get Up, Stand Up…" (Lesson 6).

3. **If no one else sees me being harassed, there's nothing I can do because the harasser will just say I'm lying.**

- It is important to speak up because the harasser may have targeted others, and all of the combined stories may establish credibility.

- Unlike sexual harassment in the workplace, which is often a "he said/she said" dispute, sexual harassment in schools usually isn't a private event since schools are very public places with many bystanders, and passers-by.

- Clearly, though, some interactions between students occur privately; students hold private conversations and may have contact with one another which is unobserved. In this instance, if two students interpret one event in different ways, the disagreement might result in one student accusing the other of "lying." That is no reason not to speak up — to tell someone whom you trust. It is also a good idea to write everything about the event that you can remember: where it took place, what time of day, what exactly happened and what was said. Write how you felt, too. These details can help with the investigation.

- Working with an adult in the school, this might be an appropriate time to "write a letter to the harasser."

- Note: See the activity and handout "Send a Letter to the Harasser" (Activity 1).

4. **If I've flirted with this person in the past, then I asked to be sexually harassed.**

- See comments regarding Question 1, above.

- Flirting and sexual harassment are two very different interactions. Flirting is a mutual encounter, stems from attraction and interest, and makes both individuals feel good. Sexual harassment is unwanted and unwelcomed by the target, and disrupts the educational environment.

- What was wanted attention on one day may not be

wanted on another — it often *depends,* as the "Flirting vs. Sexual Harassment" activity makes clear.

5. **Girls cannot sexually harass other girls.**

   - Recently, there have been same sex sexual harassment complaints. State and federal agencies which investigate complaints of sexual harassment in schools have issued contradictory rulings about whether same sex behaviors can be sexual harassment. Some of these rulings indicate that same sex harassment is considered to be sexual harassment.

   - Examples of same sex harassment include spreading sexual rumors, hanging sexually demeaning posters or writing sexual graffiti about another girl around the school, and spreading sexual rumors.

6. **Boys cannot be sexually harassed by girls.**

   - Yes, they can, and the June 1993 Harris Poll, commissioned by the AAUW Foundation, found that 57% of boys who have been harassed have been targeted by a girl, 35% by a group of girls.

   - The kinds of examples boys give include comments on the size of their private parts, jokes about the extent of their sexual experience, being called "gay," and unwanted grabbing of their butts.

   - Despite permission from the law, boys may be less likely to name behaviors as "unwanted or unwelcomed" because of social and cultural pressures.

7. **If a girl wears a short skirt or tight jeans, she is asking to be sexually harassed.**

   - Of course, girls (and boys) like to dress stylishly and attractively, but that does not mean that they want to attract everyone or that they are looking to be sexually harassed.

   - Women and girls are sexually harassed regardless of their appearance, age, race, class, occupation, or marital status. Sexual harassment is not caused by the physical characteristics of the target.

   - Sexual harassment must be distinguished from sexual attraction. Harassment is an assertion (in a sexual manner) of hostility and/or power.

- This statement is an example of "blaming the victim."

8. Girls' bodies are the only thing that matters to most boys.

- This statement is an example of gender bias and sexist stereotyping. It assumes that boys are not interested in relating to girls in caring, intellectual, friendly ways.

9. A boy who claims he has been sexually harassed is a nerd, wimp, sissy, or "wuss."

- There indeed may be strong cultural and social pressure on boys not to identify themselves as the targets of unwanted sexual attention, but the law makes no such distinction - - they are just as eligible as girls to say that they are the targets of sexual harassment.

10. Writing dirty things about someone on a bathroom wall in school is sexual harassment.

- School districts are required by law to take a stand against those actions, activities, pranks and expressions that create a hostile and intimidating, "poisoned" educational environment. When a particular student or group of students is singled out, such "targeted speech" (speech which targets a particular person/s) may not be protected by the First Amendment.

- Note: A review of an incident involving sexual graffiti is included in the case study "Katy and the Bathroom Wall" (Lesson 5).

11. If sexual harassment happens in your school, the school district can be sued in court.

- School district officials are responsible under Title IX and other federal and state statutes to guarantee all students an education in an environment free from sexual harassment and sex discrimination. It is the responsibility of school administrators to tell students the rules and explain what is legal and illegal within the school.

- If school officials are negligent and fail to respond to complaints of sexual harassment, then they are allowing and encouraging behaviors which are both frightening and illegal.

A student may file a complaint with the Office for Civil Rights of the U.S. Department of Education, which will conduct an investigation; students also may file lawsuits in federal court under Title IX.

- In a 1992 unanimous ruling, the Supreme Court established that schools may be liable for compensatory damages in sex discrimination and sexual harassment cases.

- Note: School policies and procedures, as well as students' legal rights, are reviewed in the activity "What Are Your Rights?" (Lesson 4).

12. When a girl says "no," she really means "yes" or "maybe" or "later."

- "No" means no, but sometimes people will say or do things that *mean* "no" without directly saying so. This can be confusing to the other person. For example, boys often don't understand that when a girl says, "I don't feel like it," she means "no."

- When there is the slightest doubt about whether a person is comfortable with your behavior, you must ask them what they are feeling and then *respect their limits.* Otherwise, you are pressuring someone to do something against their will, and could run the risk of committing sexual harassment, sexual assault, or some other violation of their rights.

- It is okay for a girl (or a boy) to say, "I'm not sure."

- (Some of the above material is from the *Preventing Teen Dating Violence* curriculum by Carole Sousa, Lundy Bancroft and Ted German. See the Bibliography in Chapter 5 for information on how to purchase a copy of the curriculum.)

13. If a girl says she is being sexually harassed and the boy says he is only fooling, then it's not sexual harassment.

- Sexual harassment is defined from the target's perspective, not the harasser's.

- Consensus between the target and perpetrator is unnecessary in determining the nature of a behavior. All legal definitions of sexual harassment build in personal, subjective components.

- If you do not want or welcome attention which is of a sexual nature, and if this attention is interfering with your ability to do your school work, you are being sexually harassed.

14. Sexual harassment isn't a serious problem in school since it only affects a few people.

- A majority of students report that at sometime in their school life they experience some form of sexual harassment.

- *Secrets in Public: Sexual Harassment in Our Schools,* a 1993 report written by the Wellesley College Center for Research on Women and cosponsored by the NOW Legal Defense and Education Fund, found the following results from a *Seventeen* magazine survey of girls:

  89% of girls report having received sexual comments, gestures or looks, while 83% of girls report having been touched, grabbed or pinched.

  When sexual harassment occurs, it is not a one-time-only event: 39% of girls reported being harassed at school on a daily basis during the last year.

  Sexual harassment is a public event; other people are present at over two-thirds of the incidents.

  Most harassers of girls are male.

  Note: 4300 girls between the ages of 9 and 19 responded; the study analyzed a random sample of 2000.

- *Hostile Hallways,* a 1993 survey conducted by the Harris Poll and sponsored by the American Association of University Women (AAUW) Foundation, reported the following results:

  4 out of 5 students report having been the target of sexual harassment during their school lives. Despite the stereotype of males as harassers, significant numbers of boys (76%) report having been sexually harassed, compared to 85% of the girls.

  Two-thirds of students have been the targets of sexual comments, jokes, looks or gestures.

  Over one-half of students report having been touched, grabbed or pinched in a sexual way at school.

More than one-third of students have been the target of sexual rumors.

One in ten students have been forced to do something sexual at school other than kissing.

Note: This poll was a scientific random sample of 1600 students in 8th through 11th grades.

15. If you ignore sexual harassment, it will probably stop.

- Sexual harassment which is ignored often escalates.

- Sometimes people who are being harassed are afraid to say "stop!" They may fear the harassment is their fault, or that if they mention it to someone else they'll be laughed at, retaliated against, or shamed.

- It is important for targets of sexual harassment to take some action in order to let the harasser know that his or her attention is unwanted and to alert other people — a friend, a school counselor, a trusted adult — to the problem.

- Targets of sexual harassment need to know that their *rights* are being violated and that there are concrete steps that they can take to protect themselves.

- Note: Ways for the target and others to respond to sexual harassment are reviewed on the student handout "What Can I Do?," included in the "What are Your Rights" lesson (Lesson 4); and on a second handout "Get Up, Stand Up for Your Rights," included in the "Get Up, Stand Up…" lesson (Lesson 6).

16. Boys are sexually harassed just as often as girls.

- Boys are not sexually harassed as often as girls, but a significant number of boys report having been the target of sexual harassment in school.

- The 1993 Harris Poll/AAUW Survey *Hostile Hallways* reports the following:

  Boys most commonly experience being the target of sexual comments, jokes, gestures or looks (56% of the boys, compared with 76% of the girls).

  Two of five boys (42%) have experienced being touched, grabbed or pinched in a sexual way, compared with 65% of the girls.

Roughly equal numbers of boys and girls say they have been shown, given or left sexual pictures, photographs, illustrations, messages, or notes (31% of the boys, 34% of the girls).

Twice as many boys as girls have been called "gay" ("fag," "queer").

Boys are most often harassed by a girl acting alone.

Boys are more likely than girls to have been targeted in the locker rooms and the rest rooms.

Boys are less likely than girls to tell someone they have been sexually harassed.

Objectives

To define sexual harassment; to review school district policy and procedures on sexual harassment; to inform students of their legal rights; to review possible ways for targets of sexual harassment to respond.

Background Information

 Before class, find out whether or not the school district has policies and procedures on sexual harassment for teachers, administrators, and students. If your school district doesn't have a policy, contact the Equity Office of your state's Department of Education for copies of sample policies from other school districts.

 Review, for your information, the Supreme Court decision on the *Franklin v. Gwinnett* case, and the *USA Today* op-ed piece of May 18, 1993 written by Nan Stein. Both are included in the packet of relevant readings.

 Review, for your information, the following "Background Teaching Notes" on laws regarding sexual harassment.

Preparation

 Photocopy and distribute the following student handouts "What is Sexual Harassment?" and "What Can I Do? Tips If You Feel You are the Target of Sexual Harassment."

 Photocopy and distribute written school policies and procedures on sexual harassment, if available.

Review

 Ask students to read aloud each point on the "What is Sexual Harassment?" handout. Review each paragraph carefully, helping students define any difficult words. Students may be asked to circle words they do not understand, and highlight/underline words they think are key to each point.

 Option: when reading down the list of examples of sexual harassment in school, ask several students to spontaneously role-play the incidents and ask others, as bystanders, to respond.

You may want to inform students of the etymology of the word "harassment." In old English the verb "to harass" literally meant "to set a dog on someone." Thus, the viciousness and power aspects of sexual harassment are inherent in the word's etymology.

 When reviewing the "What Can I Do?..." handout, ask students to think of (or write on a piece of paper) the names of three people they trust and who would believe them if they were sexually harassed.

 Inform students of school district policies and procedures on sexual harassment (review student handbooks, if available).

Possible Discussion Questions

1. If you were sexually harassed here tomorrow by someone in school, what would you do? What would you *really* do? (Some students may be uncomfortable with the likelihood that they would do nothing in response to sexual harassment. Explore the reasons why.)

2. If you *saw* someone being targeted by a harasser this afternoon, what would you do?

3. What if the target were your best friend?

4. What if the target were someone you didn't even know?

5. Under what conditions will you take a stand on someone else's behalf?

6. How does the popularity of the harasser figure into all of this? Would who the harasser is make a difference in how you'd respond?

7. Would the popularity of the target make a difference in how you'd respond?

8. How could you come to me and tell me about the incident *without* being a tattletale?

9. If you went to a school official and that person did not agree with you that you had been sexually harassed. What would you do then?

WHAT IS SEXUAL HARASSMENT?

☑ **Sexual harassment is unwanted and unwelcomed sexual behavior** which interferes with your right to get an education or to participate in school activities. In school, sexual harassment may result from words or conduct of a sexual nature that offend, stigmatize, demean, frighten, or threaten you because of your sex.

☑ **Agreement isn't needed.** The target of sexual harassment and the perpetrator (the one doing the harassing) do not have to agree about what is happening. Sexual harassment is subjective, defined by the person being targeted himself or herself. You do not have to get others to agree with you.

☑ **Sexual harassment can happen once or many times.** Being the target of sexual harassment may make it very scary to go to school or hard to concentrate. Incidents of sexual harassment may cause the target to feel uncomfortable, embarrassed, or threatened.

☑ **School district officials are legally responsible** to guarantee an education for all students in a safe environment which is free from sexual harassment and sex discrimination.

☑ **Some forms of sexual harassment are also crimes** and should be reported to the police or district attorney so that the perpetrator(s) can be prosecuted.

Examples of Sexual Harassment in Schools

- ◑ touching, pinching, and grabbing body parts
- ◑ being cornered
- ◑ sending sexual notes or pictures
- ◑ writing sexual graffiti
- ◑ making suggestive or sexual gestures, looks, jokes, or verbal comments (including "mooing," "barking" and other noises)
- ◑ spreading sexual rumors or making sexual propositions
- ◑ pulling someone's clothes off
- ◑ pulling your own clothes off
- ◑ being forced to kiss someone or do something sexual
- ◑ attempted rape and rape

Flirting or Hurting?, p. 37. ©1994 National Education Association and Wellesley College Center for Research on Women. Originally appeared as "Stop Sexual Harassment in Schools," by Nan Stein in USA Today (May 18, 1993): 11A.

WHAT CAN I DO?

Tips for Students If You Feel You Are the Target of Sexual Harassment

☑ **Let the harasser know** you don't like the behavior or comments. If you feel safe and comfortable doing so, tell the harasser that his or her behavior bothers you and that you want it to stop.

☑ **Tell someone and keep telling** until you find someone who believes you. Find supporters and talk with them about what's happening. The point is to find someone you can trust, and someone who will take the kinds of actions you want.

☑ **Do not blame yourself** for sexual harass-

ment. Harassment is unwanted and can make you feel trapped, confused, helpless, frustrated, embarrassed, and scared. You certainly did not ask for any of those feelings.

☑ **Keep a written record** of the incidents: what happened, when, where, who else was present, and how you reacted. Save any notes or pictures you receive from the harasser.

☑ **Find the official person** who has been designated by your school district as the one responsible for dealing with complaints about sexual

harassment. If you feel uncomfortable talking to the designated person, go to another adult whom you like and trust. It's okay to bring a friend or a parent with you to that meeting.

☑ **Write a letter to the harasser** that describes the behaviors which you consider to be sexual harassment, saying that these behaviors bother you and that you want them to stop. Keep a copy of your letter. Write the letter with the help of an adult advocate and have the adult hand-deliver the letter to the harasser so that the harasser takes this letter seriously.

☑ **You have the right to file a complaint** with the U.S. Department of Education's Office for Civil Rights, with your state's Department of Education, or to bring a lawsuit under federal law Title IX.

REMEMBER...

SEXUAL HARASSMENT IS AGAINST THE LAW!

Education

Sexual harassment in public schools is a form of sex discrimination, and therefore is prohibited by federal and state laws. Title IX of the Federal Education Amendments of 1972 (20 U.S.C. 1681) states, "No person in the United States shall, on the basis of sex, be excluded from participation in, be denied the benefits of, or be subjected to discrimination under any education program or activity receiving federal financial assistance." In addition, many states have their own laws about sex discrimination and sexual harassment in education.

Sexual harassment is defined as unwanted and unwelcomed behavior of a sexual nature. All legal definitions of sexual harassment enable the recipient (i.e., target/victim) of the behaviors to define whether the attention is unwanted and unwelcomed. This subjective component is built into the Equal Employment Opportunity Commission (1980) and the Office for Civil Rights (1981) definitions of sexual harassment, as well as into state laws and executive orders issued by governors. The presence or absence of sexual harassment thus depends on the target/victim's perception of "unwelcomed" sexual behavior.

Sexual harassment can cover a range of behaviors, including sexual insults and name-calling; off color jokes; intimidation by words or actions; offensive touching such as tickling, pinching, patting or grabbing; pressure for sexual activity; assault; and rape. Harassment may be perpetuated by peers, adults, or others with whom the target must interact in order to fulfill school or job duties. In schools, sexual harassment may be student to student, staff to student, student to staff, or staff to staff. While both females and males may be the targets of sexual harassment, in the majority of cases the target is female and the harasser is male.

An important point to remember is that sexual harassment is defined by the target. What may be hostile, humiliating, or sexually offensive to one student may not be perceived that way by another student. Therefore, when a target complains about being sexually harassed, it should not be within the purview of school staff members to decide whether or not the situation being described constitutes sexual harassment.

When the specter or hint of a sexually-tinged physical relationship between a minor and an adult in a school setting emerges, follow state law and school district policy.

In school, sexual harassment can affect a student's academic progress, extra-curricular involvement, social relationships, and self-confidence. Sexual harassment in schools that is allowed to occur unchecked can also create a school climate detrimental to the learning environment for all students. In these schools, students may not feel safe or valued as a member of the school community. Such a climate can lead to more serious sexual harassment offenses.

In February 1992, the U.S. Supreme Court issued an unanimous 9-0 decision in the *Franklin v. Gwinnett County (GA) Public Schools* case. This decision strengthened Title IX by permitting damage awards to individual targets of sex discrimination and sexual harassment (a copy of the full text of this decision is included in the "relevant reading" appendix of this guide).

Workplace

Students may want to also discuss sexual harassment in the workplace — as a current events issue, as an abstract phenomena which they may have to face later "in the real work world," and for the more obvious, relevant reason that many high school students already have jobs and may have experienced or witnessed sexual harassment at work. In addition, the subject of sexual harassment in the workplace has received enormous national attention since the Clarence Thomas/Anita Hill hearings in October 1991. Your students may remember the televised hearings or that their parents and teachers were absorbed in watching and/or discussing that watershed event.

Unlike sexual harassment in education, a legal definition of sexual harassment in the workplace has evolved from over a decade's worth of law suits. Since 1980, when the first definition of workplace sexual harassment was promulgated, court decisions have been constantly extending the application of sexual harassment. Definitions and remedies have emerged both through state and federal agencies and through the courts. What follows is only the briefest recitation of landmarks in workplace sexual harassment laws and decisions.

Title VII of the federal Civil Rights Act of 1964 prohibits employers from discriminating on the basis of sex (which includes sexual harassment) and race. Title VII is enforced by the U.S. Equal Employment Opportunity Commission (EEOC), and applies to workplaces with 15 or more employees. Title VII not only prohibits sexual harassment, but also covers retaliation against people who complain about sexual harassment and/or take out complaints.

The EEOC regulations identify three categories of conduct which constitute sexual harassment under federal law. Unwelcome sexual advances, requests for sexual favors, and other verbal and physical conduct of a sexual nature constitute sexual harassment when:

(1) submission to such conduct is made either explicitly or implicitly a term or condition of an individual's employment;

(2) submission to or rejection of such conduct by an individual is used as the basis for employment decisions affecting such individual; or

(3) such conduct has the purpose or effect of unreasonably interfering with an individual's work performance or creating an intimidating, hostile, or offensive working environment.

Sexual harassment is separated into two types: *"quid pro quo"* (which means "something for something" or "this for that"); and environmental, known as *"hostile environment."* Points (1) & (2) above would be *"quid pro quo,"* while point (3) would constitute *"hostile environment."* Quid pro quo harassment can be a single event or a series of separate incidents, and the employer is usually liable. In hostile work environment cases, usually a series of events and conduct has occurred. The employer may be liable for damages if (a) the employer knew or should have known that the harassment occurred; and (b) the employer failed to take immediate and appropriate action to correct the problem. In hostile work environment cases, the harasser can be a co-worker, a subordinate of the target/victim, a supervisor, and even a non-employee.

Targets of sexual harassment in the workplace may call upon both state and federal anti-discrimination laws. Other remedies which the target may consider include the following:

- civil lawsuits against the employer and/or harasser for assault and battery, emotional distress, wrongful discharge, breach of contract, or defamation; and

- criminal charges against the harasser for assault, rape, and other crimes.

The most important employment sexual harassment court cases include *Harris v. Forklift Systems, Inc.* (U.S. Supreme Court, November 9, 1993), and *Meritor Savings Bank v. Vinson* (U.S. Supreme Court, July 1986).

Lesson 5.
Case Studies
and Role Plays

Class Review
and Case
Presentations

(1–3 class periods)

Objectives

To grapple with the complicated factors involved in occurrences of sexual harassment; to try on the roles and respond from the perspectives of various people involved in actual cases of sexual harassment; to determine responsibility in these cases.

Preparation

☑ For day one, photocopy "Katy and the Bathroom Wall" and the supplementary readings pertaining to the case (see next page) for all students.

☑ For day two, choose and photocopy other case studies for student teams. Each team will review one case. You may use two or three different cases across the class, or assign every team the same case in order to see the variety of solutions which result. To help keep students focused, make enough copies so that each student can have his/her own copy of the team's case study.

☑ Note: All of the cases, with the exception of "The New Boy...," are based on real situations and/or actual lawsuits. The case "Susan in the Shop" may be more appropriate for senior high than junior high school students. The rest of the cases are appropriate for all students. The case "The New Boy..." deals with female-to-male sexual harassment.

Class One: Review and Discussion of "Katy and the Bathroom Wall"

☑ Hand out and read aloud the case "Katy and the Bathroom Wall" with the class. As you read down the list of recommendations following each scene, ask students to indicate one choice in a show of hands:

> "In real life, you could choose to take more than one action. But in this case, you can only make one choice. What do you think is the best thing to do?"

☑ Keep a tally of student choices on the board. Note: students may wonder why the case continues to escalate after they have made choices to better the situation. Explain that they can assume Katy does not make the same choices.

Follow with a general class discussion. Possible questions for consideration:

1. Is this a case of sexual harassment? Why or why not?

2. Assume you're a friend of Katy's and she tells you what's going on. What do you say to her, and what can you do to help out your friend?

3. Suppose you are a guy who finds the graffiti offensive. What would you say to get the other guys to stop?

4. What does the principal's phrase, "Boys will be boys," mean? Do you agree?

5. Why do you think Katy waited to tell her parents?

6. What difference might it have made if Katy had done what you suggested from the start?

Hand out copies of the supplemental Articles concerning Katy Lyle's case. Ask students to read the articles to see how the case was actually resolved.

Class Two: Team Discussion and Preparation of Other Case Studies

Divide the class into teams of 4-5 students.

Hand out copies of the same case study to students on each team. Ask each team to choose a "reader" to read the case aloud to the team, and a "recorder" to write down team answers to the questions on the back of his or her page. Give students permission to talk aloud about their case.

Tell each team to carefully consider the "bystander" question and think of two or three ways of responding as witnesses which would make the situation better.

After team discussion of cases, ask students to begin rehearsing how they would like to present their case and possible resolutions to the rest of the class (the "audience") in the next class sessions(s). No matter how authentic the students want the presentations of their case studies to be, at no time should they be permitted to engage in physical contact, intimidation, or aggression. Nor should teachers perform harassment, even when role playing a student.

Students may choose from the following formats or create a presentation of their own:

1. Teams write interior monologues or diary entries for each of the characters in the case and present these in a reading to the class.

---

2. The team creatively role-plays the case — and possible resolutions/interventions — for the class.

- Students may use real or imaginary props, costumes, a narrator, etc.

- Students may involve new characters, as well as those described in the case.

- Scenes may be set in any context: as straight reenactments, as courtroom debates, as talk show interviews, etc.

- Option: to facilitate role-playing, hand out index cards printed with the names of roles (principal, parent, older sister, target, etc.) to each team.

3. A "reporter" summarizes the case and then involves the audience (or the rest of the team) in answering the questions.

Following Class(es): Student Case Presentations

 Decide how much time you want to spend on student presentations. If there is not time for all of the groups to present their cases, remind students that everyone's participation — the audience's as well as the performers' — is important.

 Supplement student presentations with the information provided in "Background Teaching Notes" or relevant readings corresponding to several cases:

Katy and the Bathroom Wall
  "Sexual Harassment in the Boys' Room," *Choices,* (January 1993).
  "Harassment in the Halls," *Seventeen,* (September 1992).

The Playground
  "O.C.R. Urges 'Forceful' Reaction to Harassment of Children," *Education Week,* (May 12, 1993).

All-Male Varsity Kickline
  Background Teaching Notes

Optional Follow-up Activity

As a hands-on activity for younger students, ask students to make a poster illustrating what they learned from the role plays and presentations.

Katy and the Bathroom Wall

Part I.

The closest Katy had ever come to having a boyfriend had been in ninth grade. They only really spent time together on the phone. Katy considered herself a band nerd and she loved to play her saxophone. "You're such a nice girl," a senior guy named Jabari told Katy during her sophomore year, "Do you know what's written about you on the bathroom wall?" Katy's heart sank. Guys had covered two walls of a bathroom stall with really gross things about her: *Katy is a slut. Katy sucked me after she sucked my dog. Here's Katy's number. Oh, Katy, do me.* Some of the words were scratched into the wall. The next day Katy didn't want to go to school. For the next week, she cried every morning and didn't want to take the bus because guys would ask, "Are you as good as everyone says?" What would you recommend Katy do?

☐ Katy could ignore the comments.

☐ Katy could tell the boys to stop.

☐ Katy could talk to her friends about what's going on.

☐ Katy could report the incident. If so, to whom?

- one of her teachers
- a guidance counselor
- her parents
- the principal

☐ Katy could transfer to another school.

☐ Katy could file a complaint against the school district.

- If so, with whom or with what agency(ies)?

Part II.

The next week, Katy went to the principal's office to report the writing and the comments. The principal responded, "Just forget it, Katy. Boys will be boys. This is a high school, what do you expect?" What would you recommend Katy do?

☐ Katy could ignore the principal's comment.

☐ Katy could tell the principal he's wrong.

☐ Katy could talk to her friends about the incident.

☐ Katy could report the incident. If so, to whom?
- one of her teachers
- a guidance counselor
- her parents
- the superintendent of the school district

☐ Katy could transfer to another school.

☐ Katy could file a complaint against the school district.
- If so, with whom or with what agency(ies)?

Part III.

Katy decided to tell her mom and dad what was going on. Along with her parents, Katy went back to the principal and insisted that the graffiti be removed from the walls. The principal said he would take care of it, but he looked at Katy as though she had done something wrong. In fact, the principal broke his promise, and the foul language wasn't removed. The administration argued that the graffiti wasn't sexual harassment, it was merely a building maintenance problem, and they wouldn't have money in the budget to repaint the walls until the next year. Her friends noticed that Katy was becoming less outgoing and frequently saying, "My stomach hurts." Katy's grades began to drop. What would you recommend?

☐ Katy could ignore the whole issue.

☐ Katy could tell her friends what's going on.

☐ Katy could report the incident. If so, to whom?

☐ Katy could transfer to another school.

☐ Katy could file a complaint against the school district.
- If so, with whom or with what agency(ies)?

Flirting or Hurting? © 1993 Nan Stein, Wellesley College Center for Research on Women

Boys Who "Meow," and Then Some, in Class

Nikki, a 7th grade female student, goes to the principal to complain about her science teacher who hasn't noticed (or at least said anything in public) that some of the boys in the class have been staring at her, making sexual comments, and grabbing her when she passes them.

For example, one day when Nikki was making a presentation to the class, some of the boys started to "meow." The boys kept meowing softly throughout her whole speech. Nikki was distracted, to say the least, but she tried to ignore the noises and finish as quickly as she could. Other students heard the meowing, but the teacher didn't seem to notice and didn't say anything to the class.

On other days, when the teacher was moving around the classroom, some of the boys grabbed their crotches and flashed *Playboy* centerfolds at the girls. Nikki wonders why the teacher isn't doing anything to stop these behaviors. She finds these behaviors revolting and wants the principal to do something about it.

Questions

Is the "meowing" sexual harassment? Why or why not? What difference would it make if the boys were whistling? barking? mooing?

As a bystander: Suppose you were one of the other students who heard the meowing and found these behaviors to be distracting and silly. What would you do or say?

What could the teacher say or do, and at what points, that would make a difference?

Why might some boys behave in these ways toward girls?

The Playground

Every Friday was known as "Friday Flip-Up Day" in the elementary school. Any girls who wore skirts or dresses on Fridays would be fair game to have their clothes flipped up by the boys on the playground during recess. "Flip-Up Day" was well-known to parents, teachers and kids alike. It had become a kind of school tradition.

None of the adults had ever challenged the "Flip-Up Day" tradition. The girls tried to remind each other to wear pants on Fridays; anyone who forgot and wore a dress by accident would ask her teachers if she might be excused from the playground, or if she could sit out recess in the principal's office. Other girls would beg to make a telephone call to their parents to see if a pair of pants could be rushed to school in time.

One fall, "Friday Flip-Up Day" was transformed into "Pinch the Private Parts of the Girls Week." Boys chased girls around the playground, grabbing and pinching them, while shouting vulgar comments about the girls' bodies. Some of the girls' parents, outraged at this new form of playground terrorism, demanded that the school principal stop these activities.

Questions

List all of the bystanders in this situation and describe what each could have done differently to change it.

If you were a girl being targeted on the playground, how might you respond?

As a bystander: If you were an older brother or sister coming to pick up your younger sister at school and saw her being chased, "flipped," and grabbed by the boys, what would you do or say?

If you were a peer counselor to these younger girls and boys, what would you tell them? What would you say to the girls? What would be the best approaches to take with the boys?

Can little children, as young as five or six, be the targets of sexual harassment?

Can little children, as young as five or six, be harassers? Why or why not?

Flirting or Hurting? © 1993 Nan Stein, Wellesley College Center for Research on Women

The New Boy, Taunted and Targeted

Part I.

Rob has recently transferred to your school. He passes through the art corridor, a favorite hangout of the older girls. Lydia, a girl you know, and her friends Leticia and Mary rank on Rob as he passes by. You overhear Lydia remark, "Can't wait to undress you," while Leticia pats Rob's behind and comments, "Nice butt. Can I photograph you for my project?" Mary laughs the whole time and other students who are nearby, both male and female, start coming closer to see and hear what's going on. Rob mumbles something under his breath and quickly continues down the hall.

Questions

How do you think Rob feels?

In your opinion, is this an incident of sexual harassment? Why or why not?

As a bystander: You've begun to make friends with Rob and want to help him out. As you stand nearby, what are some of the different ways that you might respond (as a boy and as a girl)?

Part II.

A male teacher who saw the girls hassling Rob decides to follow him down the hall to see if he'd like to talk about the incident. When the teacher catches up to Rob away from the rest of the students, the teacher tells Rob that he's seen and over-heard everything. He asks Rob if he'd like to file an official complaint of sexual harassment against the girls. Rob replies, "You must be kidding! If a guy comes out and says he's been sexually harassed, he's going to get labeled a 'sissy' or a 'wuss.' At the same time, you like the attention and you don't."

Questions

Rob says that boys are trapped in a double-bind, liking and disliking the attention at the same time. Can you explain this? Do you think he's right?

You are a peer counselor in the school who talks with Rob. If Rob wanted to respond to the sexual harassment and protect his reputation at the same time, what would you suggest?

If you were in Rob's shoes, what would you do?

What does "sissy" mean? Who uses the word? What is it about being called a sissy that offends boys? Can girls be sissies too?

Flirting or Hurting? © 1993 Nan Stein, Wellesley College Center for Research on Women

Susan in the Shop

The Beginning

Susan, a sophomore in high school, decides to take Auto Mechanics. She is the only female in the auto shop along with 18 boys. Before signing up for the class, Susan receives encouragement from a guidance counselor whose job it is to counsel students like Susan who choose courses previously considered by many people as "sex role" nontraditional. Susan meets once a week in a discussion group with other students who also are in classes that have recently gone coed. Susan feels proud to be a girl in Auto Mechanics and happy to have this support group.

During the first week of class Susan notices that most of the boys move their chairs away from her to the other side of the room. When the first project is assigned, the guys refuse to work with Susan and one mumbles under his breath, "The bitch might break a nail and start crying." Susan is the only student who has to work alone.

Questions

Is this sexual harassment? Why or why not?

Could this situation have been avoided? How? Who's responsible?

How would you feel if you were Susan?

Why are the boys acting like this?

As a bystander: You are a boy in the class who doesn't feel good about what is happening. What can you do?

You are all members of Susan's support group, what do you say to her at your meeting?

A Few Days Later

Susan begins work on her project alone. During the week, the engine she is working on is tampered with and her tool box is hidden. Susan is scared to tell her teacher. She's afraid that if she does, the boys will become more cruel, exclude her even more, and that she'll get labeled a "tattle-tale." As much as Susan wants to be accepted by her classmates, she also wants to become an expert mechanic. Yet after the tampering, Susan can't complete her assignment properly or on time; Susan worries that she will flunk out of Auto Mechanics.

continued on next page

Questions

Is Susan being sexually harassed? Why or why not?

Who's responsible for the situation?

What can Susan do now?

As a bystander: You are one of the boys in the class. You've gone along with the others so far, but don't like how serious the situation is becoming. What can you do?

A Few Weeks Later

Several boys in the class orchestrate a special day they call "National Sexual Harassment Day." The boys pinch and pat Susan when the teacher's back is turned. They whisper dirty comments in Susan's ear. One boy pretends to slip and splashes Susan's clothes with grease. Finally, the boys lock Susan in the changing room with another male classmate. Susan is terrified and screams for help. At this point, someone unlocks the door.

Questions

Which of these behaviors are sexual harassment?

What should Susan do?

Who is responsible?

Flirting or Hurting? © 1993 Nan Stein, Wellesley College Center for Research on Women

All-Male Varsity Kickline

Part I.

Twice a year during basketball season, all of the senior, male football players lined up in a kickline to perform for the crowd during half time. Fans drove to the gym from miles around just to see them. This was no normal kickline; the varsity players dressed up as girls in elaborate costumes. The boys began by stuffing "nerf" balls under tight tee-shirts. On these "breasts," they wrote sexually provocative nicknames of girls who were on the famous, award-winning (and all-female) cheerleading squad. The boys then pulled on mini-skirts and draped brown and blond wigs on their heads. They performed several skits, all sexually suggestive and intended to mock individual cheerleaders. Most of the fans cheered on the boys.

Questions

The team members say they're "just having fun." Is this sexual harassment? Why or why not?

Your younger sister is a cheerleader in the school. She leaves the game in tears. What does she tell you later at home? How do you respond?

As a bystander: Imagine that you are sitting on the bleachers with your friends during half-time and find the kickline insulting and revolting. What can you do? At the moment? Afterwards?

Part II.

Last spring, pictures of the performance were printed in the school newspaper. Several faculty members were outraged and urged that the kickline be stopped. A female high school student and her mother wrote a letter of complaint to the school administration questioning the sexually harassing nature of the activity: "If my daughter and her friends stuffed socks down their jeans, pinned names to their crotches, and performed a skit before the entire student body mocking guys on the football team, do you think you would allow it to continue?"

Questions

How would you answer the mother and daughter's question? If the kickline were making fun of students with physical disabilities, how do you think the crowd would react?

You and your friends start a letter-writing campaign to the editor of the school paper that printed the photos. What do you write?

You and your friends decide to go further with your complaint by contacting members of the school board. What are your exact demands? What are the grounds for your demands and how do you back these up?

Flirting or Hurting? © 1993 Nan Stein, Wellesley College Center for Research on Women

Sexually harassing speech (which includes "symbolic speech" such as posters, pin-ups, lists, plays, skits and the like) may not be permitted and protected by the First Amendment if this sexually harassing speech interferes with a student's right to receive equal educational opportunities and an education that is free of sex discrimination.

School districts are required by law to take a stand against those actions, activities, pranks and expressions that create a "poisoned" (i.e., hostile and intimidating) educational environment, to punish the perpetrators, and to (re)create a school environment which is just, safe, and free from sex discrimination and sexual harassment. Furthermore, the First Amendment cannot be used as an excuse to permit blatantly sexist and misogynist material to be performed at school-sponsored events.

One particularly egregious example has occurred for generations at a high school in the mountain west. As part of a weekly school pep rally, members of a male sports team dress up in drag, don wigs and skirts, and insert nerf balls into their shirts. The boys then write the names of various girls on their shirts. This activity is school-sponsored and held in the high school. It was not until several female editors of the student newspaper in 1990 and 1991 articulated their objections to this long-standing tradition, concurrent with the arrival of a new principal, the school's first female principal, that the custom was challenged. At first, certain members of the school board threatened to fire the principal if she terminated the activity. Despite their threats and other hostile gestures directed towards her at school and at her home, the new principal put an end to this public and officially sanctioned harassment of young women in school. However, within two years she was fired from her job. The kickline has since resumed.

(For more information on this case and other court cases and complaints, see Nan Stein's working paper #256, "Secrets in Public: Sexual Harassment in Public (and Private) Schools" (1993). Wellesley College Center for Research on Women, Wellesley, MA.)

Lesson 6.
Get Up,
Stand Up for
Your Rights

A Brainstorm and Action Planning

(one class period)

Objectives

To discuss strategies to eliminate sexual harassment; to explore what it means to be a justice-maker and to respond proactively when a situation needs righting.

Preparation

Photocopy the handout "Get Up, Stand Up, Stand Up for Your Rights" for students. Hand this out *after* students have finished brainstorming.

Brainstorm

 Encourage students to see themselves as activists:

"You now recognize and know how to define sexual harassment. Noting injustice and harassment in our school is an important first step, but it's not enough. The challenge now is to take action to change conditions for the better, and you can be powerful activists who create justice in the world by beginning right here in this school."

 Ask students to brainstorm answers to the question, "What can you do to end sexual harassment in our school?"

 List students' ideas on the board or on a sheet of newsprint. If students become stumped, offer suggestions, e.g.:

1. How could you manage to make it seem 'uncool/stupid' to write graffiti on the desks and in the bathroom stalls?

2. How could you figure out ways to get boys to stop making comments about girls' bodies?

3. How could you convince the principal to take sexual harassment seriously?

4. How could you manage to get your parents involved?

5. As bystanders, how could you begin to help?

 After students have finished, distribute and read through the handout, reviewing other possible action steps to take.

 Ask students (individually, in small groups, or as a class) to consider all of the possible actions and decide upon the *three* they think are best and that would create the most change for the better in school. Ask students to write down their choices on the bottom or back of the handout.

Action Planning

Action is only effective if taken! After students have chosen three action steps, ask them to commit to following through on one or more actions and to decide if they want to do "activist work" individually, in groups, or as a class.

Discuss how to prepare for action, how to gather vital information, schedule meeting times, etc., and ask students to determine needed preliminary steps. These might include the following:

1. Find out the submission deadline for newspaper articles.
2. Find out the date of the next faculty meeting and request time on the agenda.
3. Find out the dates of school board meetings, and call to request a time on the agenda.
4. Find out the names of state legislators who chair the Education Committee, and call to set up a meeting.
5. Design signs to post around the school announcing a student task force/discussion group on sexual harassment.

Help students determine deadlines for their preliminary steps and "timelines for action."

take action...

GET UP, STAND UP STAND UP FOR YOUR RIGHTS!

Whether or not you have ever been the target of an harasser, you can stand up against sexual harassment as something you don't want happening in your school, to you, your friends, your siblings, or your peers!

There are countless ways to take action. Be creative, take courage, and involve others! All of the actions listed below you can take alone, with a friend, or with a group of "allies" — peers and/or adults.

 Write a guest editorial column or letter to your school and local newspapers.

 Attend school board meetings in your town or city and speak up about sexual harassment in your school. Inform the larger community about the issue and what you think should be done in response.

 Gather together a group of supporters and erase offensive writing from school walls, desks, lockers, etc.

 If you are the target or you see someone being harassed, speak up! Tell the harasser you don't like what they're doing. Or tell an adult you trust in the school or at home. Offer your support to the target — whether you know the person or not.

 Organize a discussion group about sexual harassment in school. This can include both students and adults.

 Volunteer to be on a task force or other committees in your school that deal with issues of sexual harassment and other student rights.

 If your school district doesn't have a sexual harassment policy in place, organize a group of interested students and schedule a meeting with the Principal to ask that s/he implement a policy. Remind the Principal that s/he has an obligation under the law to stop sexual harassment.

 Speak up about sexist language you hear in the classroom and read in books.

 If you are the target of sexual harassment, write a letter to the harasser with the help of an adult staff person whose job it is to help in these cases.

 Perform skits for other classes which focus on typical sexual harassment incidents.

 Conduct a survey on sexual harassment in your school. Use the Seventeen magazine survey (September 1992) designed by the Wellesley College Center for Research on Women.

Objectives

To explore what it means to be a justice-maker; to remind students that they have had the experience of proactively responding when a situation needed righting.

Assignment

Ask students to write about a time in their lives when they stood up for what was right. This writing may take the form of a personal narrative, illustrated poem, two- or three-act play, etc.

Debriefing

 bell hooks writes of "reclaiming a personal legacy of defiance." This process is critical not only for African-Americans, but for everyone who wishes to change things for the better. In order to stand up for our human rights and against personal injustice — be this in the form of sexual harassment, insult, ridicule, violence, or any form of discrimination — each of us needs to see and experience ourselves as powerful moral agents for what is right, rather than as moral bystanders who have no power to change the course of events.

Ask student volunteers to read their essays to the class, ask the class to listen for the courage it takes to stand up and, in a sense, defy the pressure to walk away "in innocence." Consider linking students' personal narratives with a discussion of other relevant "justice-makers" from history, literature, or current events.

Possible questions for discussion:

1. What allowed you to do this, to take a stand for what was right?

2. How did you feel?

3. We all have had (erratic) experiences of being courageous, defiant, and just. What would it take for you to become more consistently so?

The bell hooks quotation taken from Talking Back, Thinking Feminist, Thinking Black, by bell hooks (South End Press, Boston, MA, 1989), p.9.

CHAPTER 4. SUPPLEMENTAL ACTIVITIES

Activity 1.
Send a Letter
to the Harasser

A Review
and In-class
Writing
Assignment

(one class period)

Objectives

To inform students about a possible way to respond if they are targets of sexual harassment.

Preparation

 Review the following "Background Teaching Notes" describing the merits of and rationale for sending a letter to the harasser, as well as the particular elements of such a letter.

 Photocopy the sample letter for students.

Discussion

 Distribute copies of the sample letter to the class.

 Explain to students that writing a letter to the harasser (another student) is one effective way to respond after an incident of sexual harassment, and it may discourage escalation of the behavior.

 Ask for a student volunteer to read the sample letter aloud. Option: set up three chairs in front of the class, ask two students to pretend to be Susan and Richard (in the letter), and you pose as the adult advocate.

 Point out specifics to students from your review of the "Background Notes":

1. The particular form of the letter
2. The need for an adult to supervise and to act as an advocate
3. Possible ways to deliver the letter

Follow with a discussion of what the letter would accomplish. Some possible questions:

1 How could this letter make a difference?
2. Who would the letter help?

3. If you were the target of sexual harassment, how would writing this letter help you?

- Emphasize that writing a letter to the harasser is *optional*. Targets of harassment are not responsible for ending harassment (thus being re-victimized) — the school administrators are responsible!

Activity

Ask students to join in pairs and write their own letter to the harasser from the perspective of the target from one of the preceding case studies, e.g.: a cheerleader from the "All-Male Varsity Kickline" or Rob from "The New Boy…." One student takes on the role of the target, and the other the role of a peer counselor or an adult advocate.

Sample Letter for Student-to-Student Harassment

Dear Richard,

I am writing to let you know how it's been to be in auto mechanics with you—some of the things that happened between us this year, how it felt to be in class with you, and what I want to happen from now on.

When I think back to the beginning of class a few things are very clear in my memory:

1) The first week, when I started talking to you or someone else, you made cracks about me being pretty hard up if taking auto mechanics was the only way I could meet boys, or saying that maybe I was a "lezzie."

2) The next few weeks, I came into class and found my project wrecked or my tool box missing. You were always across the room watching and laughing.

3) The week of Halloween you began to threaten me that you and the other guys in class were going to pinch or grab me.

4) Then you pretended to slip and splashed me with grease.

5) The Tuesday before Thanksgiving we were locked in the changing room together and I'm sure it wasn't an accident. If Mr. Barnes hadn't heard me scream and unlocked the door, I don't know what would have happened.

Just to write these things down makes me remember how scared and lonely I always felt. So many days I would go home and cry for hours. I don't think you know how much it bothered me, and how rotten it made me feel. I'm like you Richard—I love cars and to tinker with things. Being a girl doesn't make things all that different

I'd like you to think about how you'd feel if your sister or your girl-friend told you that some guys did to her what you've done to me. I'm sure you wouldn't feel very good about this situation—I don't feel very good about it either. So, here's how I'd like you to change. First, I'd like you to treat me as a kid in the class who likes the work, is good at certain things, and just happens to be a girl. Second, stop daring the guys to tease me or touch me, since they do what you say. Third, I want you to stop teasing me, threatening to touch me, and interfering with my work.

I hope maybe things will change now that you know how I feel.

Susan

cc: J. Smith, Title IX Coordinator, Guidance Office

Flirting or Hurting?, p. 60. ©1994 National Education Association and Wellesley College Center for Research on Women

Originally appeared in Nan Stein, ed., Who's Hurt and Who's Liable: Sexual Harassment in Massachusetts Schools (Massachusetts Department of Education, 1982/1986); "No Laughing Matter: Sexual Harassment in Schools" by Nan Stein in Transforming A Rape Culture, edited by Buchwald, Fletcher and Roth (Milkweed Editions, Minneapolis, MN; 1993).

Sending a Letter to the Harasser

Writing a letter to the student harasser is a step toward taking some control over situations that often cause depression, fear, bewilderment, anxiety, and anger in the target of sexual harassment. Thus, the act of letter writing is positive and even therapeutic because it is proactive.

Unfortunately, sending a letter to the harasser does not mitigate the negative collective learning that has already occurred among the bystanders who witnessed or heard about the sexual harassment incident. For that reason, letter writing should in no way be seen as a strategy to prevent or eliminate sexual harassment in general; it will not take the place of strategies such as training programs, support groups, discipline codes, and grievance procedures.

Letter writing is not a good option in certain cases, such as when the target of harassment alleges that the harasser is a school employee, or if a student peer — the alleged harasser — is particularly anti-social.

Letter writing is an option for the target — s/he should decide if this a tactic to pursue. School personnel should not require the target to write a letter. Additionally, in order to send a letter to the harasser, the target must know the perpetrator and/or be able to identify the harasser.

Several assumptions underlie the rationale of sending a letter to the harasser:

1. It is an active response to the sexual harassment by the target.
2. It changes the balance of power: the target of the sexual harassment becomes proactive and the harasser is placed in a "receiver" role.
3. It shows the harasser there are consequences to these behaviors that live beyond the time of the incident.
4. It catches the harasser alone. The letter should be given to the harasser by the target (if he or she chooses) in the presence of an adult staff member, preferably in the privacy of the adult staff member's office. If the target would prefer not to be present, then the alleged harasser should be handed the letter in private by the adult.
5. The letter forces the harasser to face up to behaviors in a differ-

ent context from the one in which the harassment was committed — in the adult's office.

6. It allows the target to feel safe; the harasser is confronted, yet not in a face-to-face situation.

7. The letter serves the purpose of documenting the incident, the specific behaviors, the presence of witnesses, and the target's feelings. It also serves to give the harasser "fair warning" to stop.

8. It helps to contain the incident of sexual harassment among a small group of people—the target, the adult advocate, and the alleged harasser.

The letter is usually written in three parts. The first part includes a statement of the dates and facts: "This is what I think happened…"

The second part should describe the target's feelings, and what damage s/he thinks has been done. Appropriate statements in this section include opinions, feelings, anxieties, and worries, such as: "Your action made me feel terrible;" "I am scared that I'm going to be blamed for your behavior;" and "You have caused me to ask for a transfer (drop out of class)."

The third and final part of the letter should contain a short statement of what the target would like to have happen next. Statements such as these would be appropriate here: "I want those behaviors of yours to stop because they make me feel awful, and they interfere with my concentration in class and with my homework … my grades have been falling."

Portions of background notes taken from "No Laughing Matter: Sexual Harassment in K-12 Schools," by Nan Stein, in Transforming A Rape Culture, *edited by Buchwald, Fletcher and Roth (Milkweed Editions, Minneapolis, MN; October 1993). Based on "Dealing with Sexual Harassment," by Mary P. Rowe, Harvard Business Review 59, no. 3 (May-June 1981), pp. 42-46.*

Objectives

To understand the value of speaking out publicly about sexual harassment.

Preparation

 Photocopy for students the five press conference statements written and read publicly by young women in high school.

Activity

 Distribute the press statements and ask for student volunteers to read several of these aloud. Explain that one statement was a school newspaper column a girl wrote anonymously.

 Possible discussion questions:

1. What would it take to speak up publicly about incidents of sexual harassment?

2. If a girl (or a guy) in our own school spoke up publicly like this, what effects do you think this public disclosure would have on our school community?

3. Why do you think one girl decided to leave her name off of the school newspaper article?

4. If you were being sexually harassed, would you speak up in a similar way? Why or why not?

5. In your opinion, would it be harder for a girl or for a guy to speak up publicly about sexual harassment? How come?

Statement on Sexual Harassment in Schools: Tina's Story

At ten o'clock on a Monday in late December, I was lying on the floor in front of my locker writing an English paper. Words are my weapons, and I chose them carefully, defending my ideas, building my case. Deep in thought, I didn't take any notice of the guy walking past me until he had called out something in my direction. It sounded like "You waiting for someone to screw you?" I looked up and asked, "What did you say?" He repeated it, derisively. "No. I'm writing my English paper. It's good too," I answered, trying to sound strong and self-confident. I didn't want him to know how much what he had said had bothered me. It's not like I've never been harassed before—far from it—but this was more explicit than most comments, and it really unnerved me. I shook it off as well I could, though, and tried to recall my interrupted train of thought. I had begun to write again when, vaguely, I heard footsteps coming down the hall towards me. I was thinking in the back of my mind that it must be him returning from the bathroom when I felt, through my thin cotton skirt, the hard tip of a shoe brush against the back of my thighs where they join my body. I heard his voice, soft and taunting, "You waiting for someone to touch you there?" As he walked away, he sneered, "I'll touch you there."

I was stunned. While I have put up with verbal sexual harassment for years, this was the first time it had ever crossed the border into the realm of the physical. The blatant intrusiveness of this act shocked me into realizing that I can't afford to ignore the problem of sexual harassment any longer. So once again, I use words as my weapons. I've stayed silent too long, but now I'm speaking out—for myself, and also on behalf of everyone else who has been violated in this way. Because for each incident reported, there are countless others that go unaddressed. And in this case, what we don't know can be very hurtful. Sexual harassment is not something to be taken lightly.

An article in our school newspaper once defined it as "when somebody makes a move on you and you don't want them to or when somebody follows you to your house and persistently makes you feel uncomfortable." This is an example of a prevalent misconception about sexual harassment. Despite its name, it actually has less to do with sex than power. For instance, the guy that harassed me was obviously not interested in me sexually. All he was interested in was making me feel uncomfortable and intimidated. He just used sexual words and gestures to accomplish this. And it worked; I felt violated, as would anyone in that situation. What was especially scary about it was that he actually made contact with me—or rather to me—but verbal and written harassment are also frightening and humiliating. No one should have to put up with this kind of treatment. We need to start confronting the problem of sexual harassment. People like the guy who harassed me have to realize that doing what he did is unacceptable. We must send them the message that they will have to change their behavior. We have all been silent for too long, and the problem will not go away until we are willing to begin talking about it.

– Tina Blanco, 15
Acton-Boxborough Regional High School, Acton, MA

Flirting or Hurting?, p. 64. ©1994 National Education Association and Wellesley College Center for Research on Women Originally presented at Seventeen press conference (March 1993)

Statement on Sexual Harassment in Schools: Adeleine's Story

The music had just played; seventh period had just ended which meant that school was over. As I walked down the hall to meet my friend at her locker, a group of boys walked toward me. A few of them said "hello" to me while one of them just grabbed my breast and said "hi." I knew all of the guys from either the track team or school itself.

The moment he grabbed my breast I did not even stop to think about anything. I was upset and felt disrespected. All I wanted to do was show him that I was upset so he would know better than to do that. I first threw my school bag down and chased down the halls to beat him up. I was so frustrated I just wanted to smack him. He knew how upset I was and he ran. Because he was a star on the track team, I never had a chance to catch him, but that was okay because I really did not want to get into a fight.

I immediately ran upstairs to my House administrator and told him everything that had happened. He listened to me and tracked the boy down. Because I don't have a "bad reputation," I was easy to be believed although the boy denied that it happened. My House administrator called the witnesses in. I hoped the boys would tell the truth, but of course I didn't think they would because it was their friend who was trouble. I was wrong. One of the boys that was with him told the exact same story that I had.

I was supported by a lot of teachers and friends. My House administrator called my mother and told her what happened. My math teacher drove me to rehearsal, which was a distance away, because I was so upset. I was offered counseling and everything. My mommy and brother came to the school to meet with the boy, his mother, the boy's and my House administrators. We all met and talked about it.

The boy finally admitted that he grabbed my breast at that meeting.

He apologized to me and he also got suspended. He was assigned counseling. I believe he meets with a group of boys at the school's Teen Health Center every week to talk about sexual harassment and rape and things like that.

I am very happy that I did something about it. Now he knows better than to disrespect me or any female. Girls get harassed all the time, but some choose not to do anything about it. Boys are going to keep on doing it if we don't put a stop to it and tell them how we feel. Some of the boys who sexually harass girls think girls like it and that's why they don't think there is anything wrong with it. When I think about this incident, I feel good that it may be easier for other girls who hear about what I did to stop taking it themselves and do something about it.

— Adeleine Rodene, Senior Cambridge Rindge & Latin High School, Cambridge, MA

Flirting or Hurting?, p. 65. ©1994 National Education Association and Wellesley College Center for Research on Women Originally presented at Seventeen press conference (March 1993)

Statement on Sexual Harassment in Schools: Star's Story

"Those High School Men"

I've grown up in college towns all my life and I've always been warned about "those college men" and what they can do or say to you, but no one has ever warned me about "those high school men" and the harm they can cause. Maybe someone should warn young women about high school men as well. The comments made in my high school in the hallways are even more painful than the comments thrown about by the guys on a college campus because they come from my peers. I go to school with them everyday, they are my friends, I go out with them and most of all I respect them.

Yet then I hear these same guys I respect say something uncalled for to a girl passing in the hallway and I wonder what is wrong. Do they not realize how much one little comment can hurt?

At our Sexual Harassment Seminar at school this year I was shocked by many of the stories the women related. One sophomore girl said she was walking down the hallway when suddenly a guy came up close to her and began singing "I like big butts..." No doubt she was completely crushed. An event like that would crush a woman. There are some parts of certain hallways girls don't want to walk by because they are afraid of the comments, afraid of what may be yelled at them in front of the rest of their peers.

I find this disgusting and shameful all at the same time. A high school student should feel safe and comfortable walking down the halls of her school. School is a place for learning and growing. Sexual harassment stops this process. We need to educate students, both men and women about sexual harassment. Both what is and what isn't sexual harassment. We need to learn to respect people for who they are and who they are trying to become, not by how they look.

— *Star MacKenzie, 16*
Amherst Regional High School,
Amherst, MA

Flirting or Hurting?, p. 66. ©1994 National Education Association and Wellesley College Center for Research on Women
Originally presented at Seventeen press conference (March 1993)

Statement on Sexual Harassment in Schools: Imani's Story

One day I was wearing a blue chiffon blouse with a gray bodysuit underneath. A friend and I were talking and while I was talking to him he was staring at my chest. When I crossed my arms to cover my chest he moved my arms down away from my chest. I asked him 'Could you please stop doing that?' and he asked back 'Why should I?' So, I said, 'Because it's making me uncomfortable.' He responded, 'Well obviously if you wore that shirt you wanted people to look at you.' I said 'No, I just like the shirt. How would you like it if a girl looked at your crotch all day?' At first he said he wouldn't mind, then he said "Well that's different because I'm wearing jeans, and they couldn't.' I don't feel that males should be allowed to objectify women that way.

— *Imani Romney-Rosa, 16*
  Amherst Regional High School,
  Amherst, MA

Statement on Sexual Harassment in Schools: Kathryn's Story

What happened to me was not unique, it was not even exceptional. I was sitting alone in study hall, when a group of boys, whom I did not know, came over to the table next to me, and began making remarks and comments to me of a sexual nature. My philosophy in cases of "ragging" has always been to ignore it, and it goes away. This case was no different, eventually they saw that there was no rise to be gotten out of me, and quit. I recognized it as sexual harassment, but as it was not continuous, and I didn't even know who they were, I didn't do anything about it. The incident bothered me for the rest of the day, not from what they had said, but what I hadn't. I am not by nature a non-confrontational person, and anyone can testify that on arguments, intellectual or otherwise, I give as good as I get, so that letting something like this go went against the grain. These boys didn't know me, and didn't care what kind of person I was, and they succeeded in making me forget that too. They made me into a victim, a role which I hate to play, and they got away with this. I think that getting school administrations to be receptive to reports of sexual harassment is very important, but not enough. While you're training boys not to harass, train girls how to deal with harassment on their own. If I had reported this incident, and tried to make someone else do something about it, I would have been even more of a victim than before. Sexual harassment is victimization, and we need to fight that feeling most of all. Open ears to reports are very important, but not enough; we need to have the ability to throw off intimidation by ourselves, knowing that there is a support structure for us if we need it.

— *Kathryn Campbell-Kibler, 16*
  Acton-Borough Regional High
  School, Acton, MA

*Flirting or Hurting?, p. 67. ©1994 National Education Association and Wellesley College Center for Research on Women
Originally presented at Seventeen press conference (March 1993)*

Homework

In the News: Student Article and Debriefing

(a writing assignment)

Preparation

Discuss with students the need for responsible writing in newspapers, and the power of the press and editorial writers to shape public opinion.

Assignment

✓ Ask students to write their own fictional newspaper article about a supposed sexual harassment incident that just recently happened and became known to the public.

✓ Provide some common starting places for all students. Set a general scene and supply several quotations. For instance, ask students to create a scenario about a younger male or female sibling or student in the school who is harassed; provide names of 3 fictitious peers, and write three quotations on the board and let students decide to whom to attribute these; e.g.:

> "She/he asked for it!"
>
> "Don't you ever mess with her/him again!"
>
> "I don't know what to do."

✓ Ask students, after reporting the incident, to state their own opinion in the article as editorial writers.

Debriefing, next class

Ask student volunteers to read their articles aloud. Discuss the choices made by characters in the articles. Follow up with basic questions like those used in the provided case studies:

1. Is this harassment? Why or why not?
2. Why did she/he respond that way?
3. If you were this character, what would you have done?
4. If you were standing nearby, what would you do?
5. Who has a different opinion than this editorial writer? Please explain.

Optional Continuations

- Collect all of the student articles into a class paper for students and visitors to read.
- Send several of the hypothetical cases and editorial commentary to the school newspaper to raise community awareness about sexual harassment.

Objectives

To raise student awareness of current issues concerning sexual harassment in the news; to ensure ongoing discussion.

Preparation

Set up a special file for articles and cartoons dealing with the topic of sexual harassment, and determine a time each month for reviewing and discussing the contents of the file.

Activity

 Ask students to keep on the lookout for any newspaper columns, magazine articles, or cartoons dealing with sexual harassment (occurring in either schools or workplaces), to cut these out, and to add them to the file.

Review the file with students monthly, or ask teams of students to summarize the articles and lead a class discussion.

Activity 4.
Straight from
the Source

An Interview

(over the course
of a week)

Objectives

To connect with an adult and hear firsthand about growing up as a man or a woman; to ask questions and draw one's own conclusions; and to learn from another's personal experience.

Note

This assignment also works well during Women's History month.

Preparation

Photocopy the following handout "Straight From the Source: An Interview."

Activity

 By a specific date, ask students to interview a man or a woman they respect from their family, school, neighborhood, workplace, or place of worship about being a man or a woman in this culture. If necessary, brainstorm with students to help them decide whom to interview. Ask students to take interview notes and to bring these to class for discussion.

Distribute and discuss the handout on the next page which lists possible questions and reviews how to set up an interview.

Debriefing

To give each student a chance to speak and focus upon his or her interview before entering the larger class discussion, ask students briefly to recap their interview experiences to one another in pairs. Students can take turns asking each other the following questions (which can be written on the board):

> "Who did you interview?"
> "What did you find out?"
> "Did anything surprise you?"

 Ask the pairs to report back to the class and describe what they learned from each other. These reports may begin a general class discussion.

 Further questions for discussion:

1. Did anyone you interviewed experience or witness sexual harassment? How did they respond?

2. Tell me about something said that surprised or angered you…

3. What has changed the most between men and women in our society?

4. What is one thing you learned in the interview that you never want to forget?

Optional In-class Writing, a Group Accordion Poem

 Divide the class into groups of six to eight students. Each group begins with one blank piece of paper on which everyone will write one line to create a poem. Ask students to take a moment to think about what stands out for them the most from their interviews. A bit of advice? A story of difficulty? An inspiring person?

 Explain the directions for writing an accordion poem and for folding the paper like a fan:

"Together, your group is going to write a poem line by line. Everyone will begin with the same line, 'A girl, a boy, a woman, a man…' The first person should write this, then add one line of his/her own underneath on the next fold. Fold the paper over so that only your line shows. Pass it to the next person, who adds a line and folds it over so only the added line shows. The last person adds his or her line and this closing: 'A girl, a boy, a woman, a man…'" Provide an example:

Line one:	A girl, a boy, a woman, a man…
Line two:	Stevie needed to be tough to survive.
Line three:	Lena's aunt taught her to speak her mind, regardless.
Line four:	Mom didn't say anything when he grabbed her, but now she would scream.
Line five:	Sam says that men are misunderstood.
Last line:	A girl, a boy, a woman, a man…

 Ask each group to read its accordion poem aloud to the class.

 Invite students to copy their poems and give them as thank you gifts to the person they interviewed.

ask someone else...

STRAIGHT FROM THE SOURCE: AN INTERVIEW

Choose a man or a woman you respect to interview about their lives, particularly their experience of growing up male or female. This person might be a family member, a friend, a neighbor, someone from your workplace, or someone in the community. Read through the rest of the page before you begin. Also add questions of your own.

Interviewing Tips:

▲ Ask a person if they would join you to talk about being a woman or a man.

▲ Set up a time and quiet place for the interview, undisturbed by people and calls.

▲ Choose the questions you will ask, and write down some of your own.

▲ Ask the most important questions first (so you won't run out of time).

▲ Listen carefully and give your interviewee your full attention.

▲ Ask "Why is that? How come?…Please tell me more" when you want to know more.

▲ Feel free to talk about your own experiences too.

▲ Jot down in a notebook specific things that stand out in your conversation.

▲ Write the bulk of your notes afterwards, a list of things to remember.

▲ Thank your interviewee for generously talking about his or her life with you.

SOME QUESTIONS TO ASK AT THE INTERVIEW

Influential Women and Men: Who has taught you the most about being a man/woman, and what did you learn from them? What women have influenced you the most in your life, and how? What men have influenced you the most, and how?

Changes: What has changed the most for women during your lifetime? What has changed the most for men during your lifetime? What has stayed the same? What one thing would you change about the way men and women relate if you could? What would you keep the same?

Advice: What do you wish someone had told you about being male/female when you were my age? What do you think I need to know?

Adult Life: What do you like the most about being a man/woman? Tell me about one or two things that are hard about being a man/woman. What can be done to change this? What do you think would be hardest if you were a (member of the opposite sex)? How could this change?

Childhood: Were you ever teased or bullied as a child? What were you teased about and what did you do? What would you do if you saw someone being teased like that now?

Sexual Harassment: Have you ever been sexually harassed? (If yes), what did you do then? What would you do now? (If no), what would you do if you were? Have you ever seen anyone being sexually harassed? If no, what would you do if you saw someone being harassed? If yes, what did you do then? What would you do if you saw a friend being harassed now?

Flirting or Hurting?, p. 72. ©1994 NEA and Wellesley College Center for Research on Women
"*Interviewing Tips*" taken from the *Working It Out* curriculum, Ms. Foundation for Women, 1993.

Objectives

To encourage creative, proactive responses to sexual harassment by third party bystanders.

Activity

 Distribute paper and pencils/colorful art supplies. Ask students to work on their own or in pairs and draw three large, contiguous boxes which will become a three-panel cartoon. Ask students to design the first box only, and to depict an incident of sexual harassment that occurs in school or at a school activity.

 Reassure students that they do not have to be a DaVinci to do this activity. Stick figures work just fine:

"Will a boy or a girl be the target of sexual harassment? What is happening and where? How will the reader know that this is harassment, and not flirting? What words, gestures or physical actions are involved? Include conversation or thoughts in 'bubbles' if you like. What will you title your panel? Write this above your box."

 Ask a student to demonstrate and draw on the board a cartoon character speaking, and then thinking.

 When students have finished and titled their cartoons, collect the papers and redistribute randomly.

 In the second box and third boxes, ask students to draw pictures of two bystanders who see the incident happening and decide to respond in two different ways: "If you were standing right next to someone being harassed like this, how would you respond?"

✓ Collect, photocopy and arrange cartoons in a class book which can be kept on a special shelf. Or ask students to submit cartoons to the school newspaper.

Optional Continuation

Invite students to role-play their cartoon scenarios.

Activity 6.
Respect

A Brainstorm and Discussion

(one class period)

Objectives

To allow students to define for themselves how they'd like to be treated by others in social situations and in general. To reinforce that we can determine our own behavior toward others and insist upon respectful treatment for ourselves.

Introduction

Explain that you are going to begin by brainstorming together two lists; and that in a brainstorm everyone offers ideas, no answer is either "right" or "wrong," and ideas can't be criticized.

Activity

 Ask either the girls or boys to answer first. Their two lists will be compared.

 Pose the general question, "How do you like to be treated by other people?"

 Write the answers given by boys and by girls in separate columns. Ask for examples of respectful behavior in various categories:

1. How do you like to be spoken to? What are positive ways to communicate?

2. Are there respectful ways for someone to disagree or get angry with you? How?

3. What about jealousy?

4. What are some physical ways of showing respect?

5. Can someone be physically scary without touching you? How?

6. How, then, can someone show you respect without touching you?

7 What kind of joking and teasing is okay with you? How can teasing be respectful?

 After the group of girls or boys has finished, ask the second group the same questions.

- Ask students to compare the two lists. How are they the same? How are they different?

Teaching Notes

Some boys may think that the way to win respect is to exert power over another person and get their own way, particularly if they think it is important to appear "tough." Acknowledge the reality of the dangers they face (perhaps physical, perhaps the threat of humiliation), as well as the pressures put on men in this society to prove themselves by exhibiting "machismo." Offer examples of alternative respectful behaviors that do not mean men are weak or have no pride. In response, you also can ask, "If respect means getting your own way, then what happens to the person you are dominating? Aren't they being abused and disrespected? What are ways two people can earn each other's respect without there having to be a loser?"

Homework

Letter to (or conversation with) A Young Friend

(writing assignment)

Objectives

To define what it means to be respected.

Introduction

"Think of a young boy or girl you know. Imagine that they are struggling with how to get along with their peers. They respect you and come to you for advice about how to live and be respected in the world as a boy or a girl. Either write down this conversation, along with your responses; or write them a special letter in response, drawing from your own experience."

Assignment

 Ask students to choose an actual or hypothetical young friend who is either a boy or a girl. You may want to stipulate a minimum or maximum length for the conversation/letter.

Collect and choose several writings to read anonymously in class the next day. Or ask for student volunteers to read their writings aloud.

CHAPTER 5. RESOURCES

Bibliography

Surveys, Reports, Videotapes, Flyers, Posters

Be a Buddy, Not a Bully, A poster available for $7.00 from the Mid-Atlantic Equity Consortium, Inc., 5454 Wisconsin Ave., Suite 1500, Chevy Chase, MD 20815. (301) 657-7741

Hostile Hallways: The AAUW Survey on Sexual Harassment in America's Schools. (1993). Available for $8.95/11.95 from the AAUW Sales Office, P.O. Box 251, Annapolis Junction, MD 20701-0251. (800) 225-9998, ext. 246

Preventing Teen Dating Violence — Three Session Curriculum for Teaching Adolescents; and *Peer Leader Training Manual.* Both by Carole Sousa, Lundy Bancroft and Ted German. Published by Dating Violence Intervention Project. (1986). Available for $15.00 and $10.00 from Transition House, P.O. Box 530, Harvard Square Station, Cambridge, MA 02238. (617) 868-8328

Secrets in Public: Sexual Harassment in Our Schools. A report on the results of a *Seventeen* magazine survey by Nan Stein, Nancy L. Marshall, and Linda R. Tropp. (1993). Available for $11.00 from the Wellesley College Center for Research on Women, Publications Department, 106 Central Street, Wellesley, MA 02181-8259. (617) 283-2510.

Secrets in Public: Sexual Harassment in Public (and Private) Schools by Nan Stein. (1993). Working paper #256. Available for $9.00 from the Wellesley College Center for Research on Women, Publications Department, 106 Central Street, Wellesley, MA 02181-8259. (617) 283-2510.

Sexual Harassment in Schools, a videotape produced by the National Education Association and The Learning Channel. Available for $15.95 plus shipping and handling from the NEA Professional Library, Box 509, West Haven, CT 06516. (800) 229-4200.

Tune In To Your Rights: A Guide for Teenagers about Turning Off Sexual Harassment. (1985). Available for $3.00 from Programs for Educational Opportunity, School of Education, #1029, University of Michigan, Ann Arbor, MI 48109-1259. (313) 763-9910

What is Sexual Harassment?; Flirting or Harassment?; Harassment? Don't Take it! Fold out pamphlets available for $32.00 per 100 from ETR Associates, P.O. Box 1830, Santa Cruz, CA 95061-1830. (800) 321-4407.

Articles

Adler, Jerry. "Must Boys Always Be Boys?" *Newsweek,* (October 19, 1992): 77.

Atkins, Andrea. "Sexual Harassment in School: Is Your Child at Risk?" *Better Homes and Gardens,* (August 1992): 32-34.

Cheevers, Jack. "Juvenile Sex Harassment." *Los Angeles Times,* (July 4, 1995): B1, 6.

Colino, Stacy. "Fooling Around or Sexual harassment?" *Parenting,* (June/July 1993): 30.

Coolidge, Shelley Donald. "In Halls of Learning, Students Get Lessons in Sexual Harassment." *Christian Science Monitor*, (September 18, 1996): 1, 8.

Easton, Nina. "The Law of the Schoolyard." *Los Angeles Times Magazine,* (October 2, 1994): 16-24.

Goodman, Ellen. "Sexual Bullies." *The Boston Globe,* (June 6, 1993): 73.

Ingrassia, Michele, with Tim Pryor and Carolyn Friday. "Boy Meets Girl, Boy Beats Girl." *Newsweek,* (December 13, 1993): 66-68.

Kutner, Lawrence. "Harmless Teasing or Sexual Harassment." *The New York Times,* (February 24, 1994): C-11.

_____. "Everybody's Teasing Me." *Parent's Digest* (Spring/Summer 1994): 34-37.

Lanpher, Katherine. "Reading, 'Riting, and 'Rassment." *MS,* (May/June 1992): 90-91.

Lawton, Millicent. "Sexual Harassment of Students Target of District Policies." *Education Week,* (February 10, 1993): 1, 15-16.

LeBlanc, Adrian. "Harassment in the Halls." *Seventeen,* (September 1992): 162-165, 170; "Harassment at School: The Truth is Out." *Seventeen,* (May 1993): 134-135.

Lewin, Tamar. "Students Seeking Damages for Sex Bias." *The New York Times,* (July 15, 1994): B12. "Students Use Law on Discrimination in Sex-Abuse Suits." *The New York Times,* (June 26, 1995): A1, 13. "Kissing Cases Highlight Schools Fears of Liability for Sexual Harassment." *The New York Times,* (October 6, 1996): 22.

Pera, Gina. "Agony of Sexual Harassment: 2 Sides" and "How Schools Handle Sexual Harassment." *USA Weekend.* "The Great Divide, Teens and The Gender Gap." (September 6-8, 1996): 12-13, 16.

Rosen, Margery D. "The Big Issue: Sexual Harassment." *Ladies Home Journal,* (September 1993): 108-118.

Rubenstein, Carin. "Fighting Sexual Harassment in Schools." *The New York Times,* (June 10, 1993): C8.

Saltzman, Amy. "It's Not Just Teasing: Sexual Harassment Starts Young." *U.S. News and World Report,* (December 6, 1993): 73-77.

Spaid, Elizabeth Levitan. "Schools Grapple With Peer Harassment." *The Christian Science Monitor,* (January 21, 1993): 3. "Sexual Harassment Found in US Schools." *The Christian Science Monitor,* (June 2, 1993): 7.

Stein, Nan. "Sexual Harassment: When Bullying Goes Too Far." *Parent's Digest,* (Spring/Summer 1994): 35.

_____. "Sexual Harassment in K-12 Schools: The Public Performance of Gendered Violence." *The Harvard Educational Review,* Special Issue: Violence and Youth (Vol.65, #2, Summer 1995): 145-162.

Organizations Working to Create More Equity in Schools

The Bill of Rights Education Project: Works with teachers to make civil liberties and civil rights relevant to students. Runs summer teacher institutes and teacher/student conferences. A free tri-annual newsletter Bill of Rights Network available from the Bill of Rights Education Project, 99 Chauncy Street, Suite 310, Boston, MA 02111; (617) 482-3170 x310.

Educators Against Racism and Apartheid: Newsletter available for $10.00 from Educators Against Racism and Apartheid, 164-04 Goethals Avenue, Jamaica, NY 11432; (201) 836-6644.

Educators for Social Responsibility (ESR): Develops curricula and trains teachers with a particular focus on conflict resolution. A Resources for Empowering Children catalogue available from ESR, 23 Garden Street, Cambridge, MA 02138; (617) 492-1764.

Facing History and Ourselves: Develops curricula and trains teachers to engage adolescents in an examination of racism, bigotry, and anti-Semitism through a study of the Holocaust. Information available from Facing History and Ourselves, 16 Hurd Road, Brookline, MA 02146; (617) 232-1595.

FairTest: A public education and advocacy organization which works on issues concerning standardized testing on K-12 and college levels. A quarterly newsletter FairTest Examiner available for $20.00 from FairTest, 342 Broadway, Cambridge, MA 02139; (617) 864-4810.

National Coalition of Advocates for Students (NCAS): A coalition of 22 child advocacy groups in 14 states. Information and a catalogue of publications available from NCAS, 100 Boylston Street, Suite 737, Boston, MA 02116; (617) 357-8507.

National Coalition of Education Activists (NCEA): A quarterly newsletter Action for Better Schools and information available from the National Coalition of Education Activists, P.O. Box 679, Rhinebeck, NY 12572; (914) 876-4580.

Network of Educators on the Americas (NECA): Develops and distributes anti-racist, multicultural curricula and books. A Teaching for Change catalogue and quarterly newsletter available from NECA, 1118 22nd Street, NW, Washington, DC 20037; (202) 429-0137.

Rethinking Schools Ltd: Publishers of *Rethinking Schools,* a quarterly activist educational journal. Subscription rates $12.50 per year. Available from Rethinking Schools, 1001 E. Keefe Ave., Milwaukee, WI 53212; (414) 964-9646.

APPENDIX: RELEVANT READINGS

Christine Franklin, Petitioner v Gwinnett County Public Schools and William Prescott

On Writ of Certiorari to the United States Court of Appeals for the Eleventh Circuit

SUMMARY: ARGUED DECEMBER 11, 1991–
DECIDED FEBRUARY 26, 1992
112 S.Ct 1028 (1992)

Practitioner Franklin, a student in a high school operated by respondent school district, filed an action for damages in Federal District Court under Title IX of the Education Amendments of 1972, alleging *inter alia,* that she had been subjected to continual sexual harassment and abuse by a teacher, Andrew Hill. After the complaint was filed, Hill resigned on the condition that all matters pending against him be dropped, and the school thereupon closed its investigation. The District Court subsequently dismissed the compliant on the ground that Title IX does not authorize an award of damages, and the Court of Appeals affirmed.

Held: A damages remedy is available for an action brought to enforce Title IX:

(a) Title IX is enforceable through an implied right of action. *Cannon v. University of Chicago,* 441 U. S. 677.

(b) The longstanding general rule is that absent clear direction to the contrary by Congress, the federal courts have the power to award any appropriate relief in cognizable cause of action brought pursuant to a federal statute. See *e.g., Bell v. Hood,* 327 U.S. 678, 684; *Davis v. Passman,* 442 U.S. 228, 246-247.

(c) This Court's adherence to the general rule has not eroded since *Bell.* See, *e.g., J.I. Case Co. v. Borak,* 377 U.S. 426, 433-435. In declaring that "the question of who may enforce a *statutory* right is fundamentally different from the question of who may enforce a [constitutionally protected] right," *Davis,* 442 U.S., at 241, was not limiting the traditional presumption in favor of all appropriate relief to actions claiming constitutional violations. Rather it was merely attempting to decide whether a litigant had a "cause of action," a question that is ana-

lytically distinct from, and prior to, the one at issue: what relief, if any a litigant is entitled to receive, see *id.,* at 239. Nor did *Guardians Assn. v. Civil Service Comm'n of New York City,* 463 U. S. 582, and *Consolidated Rail Corp. v. Darrone,* 465 U. S. 624, erode the traditional presumption. In fact, those cases support it, since a clear majority in *Guardians* expressed the view that damages were available in an action seeking remedies for an intentional violation of a statute closely analogous to Title IX while a unanimous Court in Darrows held that another such statute authorized the award of backpay.

(d) Congress did not intend to limit the remedies available in a Title IX suit. Because the *Cannon* Court inferred a cause of action upon concluding that Title IX supported no express right of action, the silence of the pre-*Cannon* statutory text and legislative history on the issue of available remedies is neither surprising nor enlightening. Rather, the appropriate inquiry for the pre-*Cannon* period is the state of the law when Congress passed Title IX. Since, at that time, the traditional presumption in favor of all available remedies was firmly established, and this Court had recently found implied rights of action in six cases and approved a damages remedy in three of them, the lack of any legislative intent to abandon the traditional presumption is amply demonstrated. For the post-*Cannon* period, when Congress was legislating with full cognizance of that decision, analysis of the text and history of the two statutes enacted to amend Title IX—the Civil Rights Remedies Equalization Amendment of 12986 and the Civil Rights Restoration Act of 1987—establishes that Congress validated *Cannon's* holding and made no effort to alter the traditional presumption.

(e) The argument that a damages award would unduly expand the federal courts' power into a sphere properly reserved to the Executive and Legislative Branches in violation of separation of powers principles misconceives the difference between a cause of action and a remedy. Unlike the finding of a cause of action, which authorizes a court to hear a case or controversy, the discretion to award appropriate relief involves no such increase in judicial power and, in fact, historically has been thought necessary to provide an important safeguard against legislative and executive abuses and to insure an independent judiciary. Moreover, selective adjudication of the sort advocated here would harm separation of powers by giving judges the power to render inutile causes of action authorized by Congress through a decision that *no* remedy is available.

(f) Also rejected is the contention that the normal presumption in favor of all appropriate remedies should not apply because Title IX was enacted pursuant to Congress' Spending Clause power. The Court's observation in *Pennhurst State School and Hospital v. Halderman*, 451 U. S. 1, 25-29, that remedies are limited under Spending Clause statutes when the alleged violation is *unintentional* is based on the theory that an entity receiving federal funds lacks notice that it will be liable for damages for such a violation, see *id.,* at 17. This notice problem does not arise in a case such as the present, where intentional discrimination is alleged and is proscribed by the statute in question. Moreover, the notion that Spending Clause statues do not authorize monetary awards for intentional violations is belied by the unanimous holding in *Darrone, supra,* at 628.

(g) The assertion that Title IX remedies should nevertheless be limited to backpay and prospective relief diverges from this Court's traditional approach to deciding what remedies are available for violation of a federal right. Both suggested remedies are equitable in nature, and it is axiomatic that a court should determine the adequacy of damages at law before resorting to equitable relief. Moreover, both suggested remedies are clearly inadequate in that they would provide Franklin no relief: back pay because she was a student when the alleged discrimination occurred, and prospective relief because she no longer attends school in respondent system and Hill no longer teaches there.

911 F. 2d 617, reversed and remanded.

WHITE, J., delivered the opinion of the Court, in which BLACKMUN, STEVENS, O'CONNOR, KENNEDY, and SOUTER, JJ., joined. SCALIA, J., filed and opinion concurring in the judgment, in which REHNQUIST, C.J., and THOMAS, J., joined.

JUSTICE WHITE delivered the opinion of the court.

This case presents the question whether the implied rights of action under Title IX of the Education Amendments of 1972, 20 U.S.C. §1681-1688 (Title IX),[1] which this court recognized in *Cannon v. University of Chicago,* 441 U.S. 677 (1979), supports a claim for monetary damages.

I

Petitioner Christine Franklin was a student at Gwinnett High School in Gwinnett County, Georgia, between September 1985 and August 1989. Respondent Gwinnet County School District operates the high school and receives federal funds. According to the complaint filed on December 29, 1988 in the United States District Court for the Northern District of Georgia, Franklin was subjected to continual sexual harassment beginning in the autumn of her tenth grade year (1986) from Andrew Hill, a sports coach and teacher employed by the district. Among other allegations, Franklin avers that Hill engaged her in sexually-oriented conversations in which he asked about her sexual experiences with her boyfriend and whether she would consider having sexual intercourse with an older man, Compliant ¶10; First Amended Complaint. Exh. A, p.3;[2] that Hill forcibly kissed her on the mouth in the school parking lot, Complaint ¶17; that he telephoned her at home and asked if she would meet him socially, Complaint ¶21; First Amended Complaint, Exh. A, pp. 4-5; and that, on three occasions in her junior year, Hill interrupted a class, requested that the teacher excuse Franklin, and took her to a private office where he subjected her to coercive intercourse. Complaint ¶¶25, 27, 32. The complaint further alleges that though they became aware of and investigated Hill's sexual harassment of Franklin and other female students, teachers and administrators took no action to halt it and discouraged Franklin from pressing charges against Hill. Complaint ¶23, 24, 35. On April 14, 1988, Hill resigned on the condition that all matters pending against him be dropped. Complaint ¶¶36, 37. The school thereupon closed its investigation. Complaint ¶37.

In this action,[3] the District Court dismissed the Complaint on the ground that Title IX does not authorize an award of damages. The Court of Appeals affirmed. *Franklin v. Gwinnett City. Public Schools,* 911 F. 2d 617 (CA11 1990). The court noted that analysis of Title IX and Title IV of the Civil Rights Act of 1964, 42 U.S.C. §2000d *et seq.* (Title VI), has developed along similar lines. Citing as binding precedent *Drayden v. Needville Independent School Dist.,* 642 F. 2d 129 (CA5 1981), a decision rendered prior to the decision of the Fifth Circuit, the court concluded that Title VI did not support a claim for monetary damages. The court then analyzed this Court's decision in *Guardians Assn. v. Civil Service Comm'n of New York City* 463 U.S. 582 (1983), to determine whether it implicitly overruled *Drayden.* The court stated that the absence of a majority opinion left unresolved the question whether a court could award such relief upon showing of intentional discrimination. As a second basis for its holding that a monetary damages were unavailable, the court reasoned that Title IX was enacted under Congress' Spending Clause powers and that "[u]nder such statutes, relief may frequently be limited to that which is equitable in nature, with the recipient of federal funds thus retaining the option of terminating such receipt in order to rid itself of an injunction." *Franklin,* 911 F. 2d, at 621.[4] The court closed by observing it would "proceed with extreme care" to afford compensatory relief absent express provision by Congress or clear direction from this Court. *Id.,* at 622. Accordingly, it held that an action for monetary damages could not be sustained for an alleged intentional violation of Title IX, and affirmed the District Court's ruling to that effect. *Ibid.*[5]

Because this opinion conflicts with a decision of the Court of Appeals for the Third Circuit, see *Pfeiffer v. Marion Center Area School Dist.,* 917 F. 2d 779, 787-789 (1990), we granted certiorari, 501 U.S. ___ (1991). We reverse.

II

In *Cannon v. University of Chicago,* 441 U.S. 677 (1979), the Court held that Title IX is enforceable through an implied right of action. We have no occasion here to reconsider that decision. Rather, in this case we must decide what remedies are available in a suit brought pursuant to this implied right. As we have often stated, the question of what remedies are available under a statute that provides a private right of action is "analytically distinct" from the issue of whether such a right exists in the first place. *Davis v. Passman,* 442 U.S. 228, 239 (1979). Thus, although we examine the text and history of a statute to determine whether Congress has intended to create a right of action, *Touche Ross & Co. v. Redington,* 442 U.S. 560, 575-576 (1979), we presume the availability of all appropriate remedies unless Congress has expressly indicated otherwise. *Davis, supra,* at 246-247. This principle has deep roots in our jurisprudence.

A

"[W]here legal rights have been invaded, and a federal statute provides for a general right to sue for such invasion, federal courts may use any available remedy to make good the wrong done." *Bell v. Hood,* 327 U.S. 678, 684 (1946). The Court explained this longstanding rule as jurisdictional, and upheld the exercise of the federal courts' power to award appropriate relief so long as a course of action existed under the Constitution or laws of the United States. *Ibid.*

The *Bell* Court's reliance on this rule was hardly revolutionary. From the earliest years of the Republic, the Court has recognized the power of the judiciary to award appropriate remedies to redress injuries actionable in federal court, although it did not always distinguish clearly between a right to bring suit and a remedy available under such a right. In *Marbury v. Madison,* 1 Cranch 137, 163 (1803), for example, Chief Justice Marshall observed that our government "has been emphatically termed a government of laws, and not of men. It will certainly cease to deserve this high appellation, if the laws furnish no remedy for the violation of a vested legal right." This principle originated in the English common law, and Blackstone described "it is a general and indisputable rule, that where there is a legal right, there is also a legal remedy, by suit or action at law, whenever that right is invaded." 3 W. Blackstone, Commentaries 23 (1783). See also *Ashby v. White*, 1 Salk, 19, 21, 87 Eng. Rep. 808, 816 (Q.B. 1702) ("If a statute gives a right, the common law will give a remedy to maintain that right...").

In *Kendall v. United States*, 12 Pet. 524 (1838), the Court applied these principles to an act of Congress that accorded a right of action in mail carriers to sue for adjustment and settlement of certain claims for extra services but which did not specify the premise remedy available to the carriers. After surveying possible remedies, which included an action against the postmaster general for monetary damages, the Court held that the carriers were entitled to a writ of mandamus compelling payment under the terms of the statute. "It cannot be denied but that congress had the power to command that act to be done," the Court stated; "and the power to enforce the performance of the act must rest somewhere, or it will present a case which has often been said to involve a monstrous absurdity in a well organized government, that there should be no remedy, although a clear and undeniable right should be shown to exist. And if the remedy cannot be applied by the circuit court of this district, it exists nowhere." *Id.*, at 624. *Dooley v. United States*, 182 U.S. 222, 229 (1901), also restated "the principle that a liability created by statute without a remedy may be enforced by a common-law action."

The Court relied upon this traditional presumption again after passage of the Federal Safety Appliance Act of 1893, ch. 196,27 Stat.531. In *Texas & Pacific R. Co. v. Rigsby*, 241 U.S. 33 (1916), the Court first had to determine whether the Act supported an implied right of action. After answering that question in the affirmative, the Court then upheld a claim for monetary damages: "A disregard of the command of the statute is a wrongful act, and where it results in damage to one of the class for whose especial benefit the statute was enacted, the right to recover the damages from the party in default is implied, according to a doctrine of the common law..." *Id.*, at 39. The foundation upon which the *Bell v. Hood* Court articulated this traditional presumption, therefore, was well settled. See also *Texas & New Orleans R. Co. v. Railway & Steamship Clerks*, 281 U.S. 548, 569 (1930).

B

Respondents and the United States as *amicus curiae*, however, maintain that whatever the traditional presumption may have been when the Court decided *Bell v. Hood*, it has disappeared in succeeding decades. We do not agree. In *J.I. Case Co. v. Borak*, 377 U.S. 426 (1964), the Court adhered to the general rule that all appropriate relief is available in an action brought to vindicate a federal right when Congress has given no indication of its purposes with respect to remedies. Relying on *Bell v. Hood*, the *Borak* Court specifically rejected an argument that a court's remedial power to redress violations of the Securities Exchange Act of 1934 was limited to a declaratory judgment. 377 U.S., at 433-434. The Court concluded that the federal courts "have the power to grant all necessary remedial relief" for violations of the Act. *Id.*, at 435. As Justice Clark's opinion for the Court observed, this holding closely followed the reasoning of a similar case brought under the Securities Act of 1933, in which the Court has stated:

" 'The power to *enforce* implies the power to make effective the right of recovery afforded by the Act. And the power to make the right of recovery effective implies the power to utilize any of the procedures or actions normally available to the litigant according to the exigencies of the particular case.' " *Id.*, at 433-434 (quoting *Deckert v. Independence Shares Corp.*, 311 U.S. 282, 288 (1940)0.

That a statute does not authorize the remedy at issue "in so many words is no more significant than the fact that it does not in terms authorize execution to issue on a judgment." *Id.*, at 288. Subsequent cases have been true to this position. See, *e.g.*, *Sullivan v. Little Hunting Park, Inc.*, 396 U.S. 229, 239 (1969), stating that the "existence of a statutory right implies the existence of all necessary and appropriate remedies."; *Carey v. Piphus*, 435 U.S. 247, 255 (1978), upholding damages remedy under 42 U.S.C. 1983 even though the enacting Congress had not specifically provided such relief.

The United States contends that the traditional presumption in favor of all appropriate relief was abandoned by the Court in *Davis v. Passman*, 442 U.S. 228 (1979), and that the *Bell v. Hood* rule was limited to actions claiming constitutional violations. The United States quotes language in *Davis* to the effect that "the question of who may enforce a *statutory* right is fundamentally different from the question of who may enforce a right that is protected by the Constitution." *Davis*, 442 U.S. at 241. The Government's position, however, mirrors the very misunderstanding over the difference between a cause of action and the relief afforded under it that sparked the confusion we attempted to clarify in *Davis*. Whether Congress may limit the class of persons who have a right of action under Title IX is irrelevant to the issue in this lawsuit. To reiterate, "the question whether a litigant has a 'cause of action' is analytically distinct and prior to the question of what relief, if any, a litigant may be entitled to receive." *Id.,* at 239. *Davis*, therefore, did nothing to interrupt the long line of cases in which the Court has held that if a right of action exists to enforce a federal right and Congress is silent on the question of remedies, a federal court may order any appropriate relief. See *id.,* at 247, n.26 (contrasting *Brown v. General Services Administration*, 425 U.S. 820 (1976)).[6]

Contrary to arguments by respondents and the United States that *Guardians Assn. v. Civil Service Comm'n of New York City,* 463 U.S. 582 (1983), and *Consolidated Rail Corp. v. Darrone,* 465 U.S. 624 (1984), eroded this traditional presumption, those cases in fact support it. Though the multiple opinions in *Guardians* suggest the difficulty of inferring the common ground among the Justices in that case, a clear majority expressed the view that damages were available under Title VI in an action seeking remedies for an intentional violation, and no Justice challenged the traditional presumption in favor of a federal court's power to award appropriate relief in a cognizable cause of action. See *Guardians,* 463 U.S., at 595 (WHITE, J., joined by REHNQUIST, J.); *id.,* at 607-611 (Powell, J., concurring in judgment, joined by Burger, C.J.); *id.,* at 612,

and n.1 (O'CONNOR, J., concurring in judgment); *id.,* at 624-628 (Marshall, J., dissenting); *id.,* at 636 (STEVENS, J., dissenting, joined by Brennan and BLACKMUN, JJ.). The correctness of this inference was made clear the following Term when the Court unanimously held that the 1978 amendment to 504 of the Rehabilitation Act of 1973—which had expressly incorporated the "remedies, procedures, and rights set forth in title VI" (29 U.S.C. §794a(a)(2)—authorizes an award of backpay. In *Darrone*, the Court observed that a majority in *Guardians* had "agreed that retroactive relief is available to private plaintiffs for all discrimination...that is actionable under Title VI." 465 U.S. at 630, n.9. The general rule, therefore, is that absent clear direction to the contrary by Congress, the federal courts have the power to award any appropriate relief in a cognizable cause of action brought pursuant to a federal statute.

III

We now address whether Congress intended to limit application of this general principle in the enforcement of Title IX. See *Bush v. Lucas,* 462 U.S. 367, 378 (1983); *Wyandotte Transp. Co. v. United States,* 389 U.S. 191, 200 (1967). Because the cause of action was inferred by the Court in *Cannon*, the usual recourse to statutory text and legislative history in the period prior to that decision necessarily will not enlighten our analysis. Respondents and the United States fundamentally misunderstood the nature of the inquiry, therefore, by needlessly dedicating large portions of their briefs to discussions of how the text and legislative intent behind Title IX are "silent" on the issue of available remedies. Since the Court in *Cannon* concluded that this statute supported no express right of action, it is hardly surprising that Congress also said nothing about the applicable remedies for an implied right of action.

During the period prior to the decision in *Cannon,* the inquiry in any event is *not* "'basically a matter of statutory construction,'" as the United States asserts. Brief for United States as *Amicus Curiae* 8 (quoting *Transamerica Mortgage Advisors, Inc. v. Lewis,* 444 U.S. 11, 15 (1979)). Rather, in determining Congress' intent to limit application of the traditional presumption in favor of all appropriate relief, we evaluate the state of the law when the legislature passed Title IX. Of *Merrill Lynch, Pierce, Fenner & Smith, Inc. v. Curran,* 456 U.S. 353, 378 (1982). In the years before and after Congress enacted this statute, the Court "follow[ed] a common-law tradition [and] regarded the denial of a remedy as the exception rather than the rule." *Id.,* at 375 (footnote omitted). As we outlined in Part II, this has been the prevailing presumption in our federal courts since at least the early nineteenth century. In *Cannon,* the majority upheld an implied right of action in part because in the decade immediately preceding enactment of Title IX in 1972, this Court had found implied rights of action in six cases.[7] In three of those cases, the Court had approved a damages remedy. See *e.g., J.I. Case Co.* 377 U.S. at 433, *Wyandotte Transp. Co., supra,* at 207; *Sullivan v. Little Hunting Park, Inc.* 396 U.S. 229 (1969). Wholly apart from the wisdom of the *Cannon* holding, therefore, the same contextual approach used to justify an implied right of action more than amply demonstrates the lack of any legislative intent to abandon the traditional presumption in favor of all available remedies.

In the years *after* the announcement of *Cannon,* on the other hand, a more traditional method of statutory analysis is possible, because Congress was legislating with full cognizance of that decision. Our reading of the two amendments to Title IX enacted after *Cannon* leads us to conclude that Congress did not intend to limit the remedies available in a suit brought under Title IX. In the Civil Rights Remedies Equalization Amendment of 1986, 42 U.S.C. §2000d-7, Congress abrogated the States' Eleventh Amendment immunity under Title IX, Title VI, §504 of the Rehabilitation Act of 1973, and the Age Discrimination Act of 1975. This statute cannot be read except as a validation of *Cannon's* holding. A subsection of the 1986 law provides that in a suit against a State, "remedies (including remedies both at law and in equity) are available for such a violation to the same extent as such remedies are available for such a violation in the suit against any public or private entity other than a State." 42 U.S.C. §2000d-7(a)(2). While it is true that

this savings clause says nothing about the nature of those other available remedies, cf. *Milwaukee v. Illinois,* 451 U.S. 304, 329, n.22 (1981), absent any contrary indication in the text or history of the statute with the prevailing traditional rule in mind.

In addition to the Civil Rights Remedies Equalization Amendment of 1986, Congress also enacted the Civil Rights Restoration Act of 1987, Pub. L. 100-259, 102 Stat. 28 (1988). Without in any way altering the existing rights of action and the corresponding remedies permissible under Title IX, Title VI, §504 of the Rehabilitation Act, and the Age Discrimination Act, Congress broadened the coverage of these antidiscrimination provisions in this legislation. In seeking to correct what is considered to be an unacceptable decision on our part in *Grove City College v. Bell,* 465 U.S. 555 (1984), Congress made no effort to restrict the right of action recognized in *Cannon* and ratified in the 1986 Act or alter the traditional presumption in favor of any appropriate relief or violation of a federal right. We cannot say, therefore, that Congress has limited the remedies available to a complainant in a suit brought under Title IX.

IV

Respondents and the United States nevertheless suggest three reasons why we should not apply the traditional presumption in favor of appropriate relief in this case.

A

First, respondents argue that an award of damages violates separation of powers principles because it unduly expands the federal courts' power into a sphere properly reserved to the Executive and Legislative Branches. Brief for Respondents 22-25. In making this argument, respondents misconceive the difference between a cause of action and a remedy. Unlike the finding of a cause of action, which authorizes a court to hear a case or controversy, the discretion to award appropriate relief involves no such increase in judicial power. See generally Note, Federal Jurisdiction in Suits for Damages Under Statutes Not Affording Such Remedy, 48 Colum.L.Rev. 1090, 1094-1095 (1948). Federal courts cannot reach out to award remedies when the Constitution or laws of the United States do not support a cause of action. Indeed, properly understood, respondents' position invites us to *abdicate* our historic judicial authority to award appropriate relief in cases brought in our court system. It is well to recall that such authority historically has been thought necessary to provide an important safeguard against abuses of legislative and executive power, see *Kendell v. United States*, 2 Pet. 524 (1838), as well as to insure an independent judiciary. See generally Katz, The Jurisprudence of Remedies: Constitutional Legality and the Law of Torts in *Bell v. Hood*, 117 U. Pa. L. Rev. 1, 16-17 (1968). Moreover, selective abdication of the sort advocated here would harm separation of powers principles in another way, by giving judges the power to render inutile causes of action authorized by Congress through a decision that *no* remedy is available.

B

Next, consistent with the Court of Appeal's reasoning, respondents and the United States contend that the normal presumption in favor of all appropriate remedies should not apply because Title IX was enacted pursuant to Congress's Spending Clause power. In *Pennhurst State School and Hospital v. Halderman*, 451 U.S. 1, 28-29 (1981), the Court observed that remedies were limited under such Spending Clause statues when the alleged violation was *unintentional*. Respondents and the United States maintain that this presumption should apply equally to *intentional* violations. We disagree. The point of not permitting monetary damages for an unintentional violation is that the receiving entity of federal funds lacks notice that it will be liable for a monetary award. See *id.,* at 17. This notice problem does not arise in a case such as this, in which intentional discrimination is alleged. Unquestionably, Title IX placed on the Gwinnet County Schools the duty not to discriminate on the basis of sex, and "when a supervisor sexually harasses a subordinate because of the subordinate's sex, that supervisor 'discriminate[s]' on the basis of sex." *Meritor Savings Bank, FSB v. Vinson*, 477 U.S. 57, 64 (1986). We believe the same rule should apply when a teacher sexually harasses and abuses a student. Congress surely did not intend for federal monies to be expended to support the intentional actions it sought by statute to proscribe. Moreover, the notion that Spending Clause statues do not authorize monetary awards for intentional violations is belied by our unanimous holding in *Darrone*. See 465 U.S. at 628. Respondents and the United States characterize the backpay remedy in *Darrone* as equitable relief, but this description is irrelevant to their underlying objection: that application of the traditional rule in this case will require state entities to pay monetary awards out of their treasuries for intentional violations of federal statutes.[8]

C

Finally, the United States asserts that the remedies permissible under Title IX should nevertheless be limited to backpay and prospective relief. In addition to diverging from our traditional approach to deciding what remedies are available for violation of a federal right, this position conflicts with sound logic. First, both remedies are equitable in nature, and it is axiomatic that a court should determine the adequacy of a remedy in law before resorting to equitable relief. Under the ordinary convention, the proper inquiry would be whether monetary damages provided an adequate remedy, and if not, whether equitable relief would be appropriate. *Whitehead v. Shattuck*, 138 U.S. 146, 150 (1891). See generally C. McCormick, Law of Damages 1 (1935). Moreover, in this case the equitable remedies suggested by respondent and the Federal Government are clearly inadequate. Backpay does nothing for petitioner, because she was a student when the alleged discrimination occurred. Similarly, because Hill—the person she claims subjected her to sexual harassment—no longer teaches at the school and she no longer attends a school in the Gwinnett system, prospective relief accords her no remedy at all. The government's answer that administrative action helps other similarly-situated students in effect acknowledges that its approach would leave petitioner remediless.

V

In sum, we conclude that a damages remedy is available for an action brought to enforce Title IX. The judgment of the Court of Appeals, therefore, is reversed and the case is remanded for further proceedings consistent with this opinion.

So ordered.

JUSTICE SCALIA, with whom the CHIEF JUSTICE and JUSTICE THOMAS join, concurring in the judgment.

The substantive right at issue here is one that Congress did not expressly create, but that this court found to be "implied." See *Cannon v. University of Chicago*, 441 U.S. 677 (1979). Quite obviously, the search for what was Congress's *remedial* intent as to a right whose very existence Congress did not expressly acknowledge is unlikely to succeed, see *ante*, at 9-10; it is "hardly surprising," as the Court says, *ibid.*, that the usual sources yield no explicit answer.

The Court finds an implicit answer, however, in the legislators' presumptive awareness of our practice of using "any available remedy" to redress violations of legal rights. *Bell v. Hood*, 327 U.S. 678, 684 (1946); see *ante*, at 10-11. This strikes me as question-begging. We can plausibly assume acquiescence in our *Bell v. Hood* presumption when the legislature says nothing about remedy in expressly creating a private right of action; perhaps even when it says nothing about remedy in creating a private right of action by clear textual implication; but not, I think, when it says nothing about remedy in a statute in which the courts divine a private right of action on the basis of "contextual" evidence such as that in *Cannon*, which charged Congress with knowledge of a court of appeals' creation of a cause of action under a similarly worded statute. See *Cannon, supra,* at 696-698. Whatever one thinks of the validity of the last approach, it surely rests on attributed rather than actual congressional knowledge. It does not demonstrate an explicit legislative decision to create a cause of action, and so could not be expected to be accompanied by a legislative decision to alter the application of *Bell v.*

Hood. Given the nature of *Cannon* and some of our earlier "implied right of action" cases, what the Courts' analytical construct comes down to is this: Unless Congress expressly legislates a more limited remedy; policy with respect to rights of action it does not know it is creating, it intends the full gamut of remedies to be applied.

In my view, when rights of action are judicially "implied," categorical limitations upon their remedial scope may be judicially implied as well. Cf. *Cort v. Ash*, 422 U.S. 66, 84-85. Although we have abandoned the expansive rights-creating approach exemplified by *Cannon*, see *Touche Ross & Co. v. Redington*, 442 U.S. 560, 575-576 (1979); *Transamerica Mortgage Advisors, Inc. v. Lewis*, 444 U.S. 11, 18, 23-24, (1979)—and perhaps ought to abandon the notion of implied causes of action entirely, see *Thompson v. Thompson*, 484 U.S. 174, 191 (1988) (SCALIA, J., concurring in judgment)—causes of action that came into existence under the *ancien regime* should be limited by the same logic that gave them birth. To require, with respect to a right that is not consciously and intentionally created, that any limitation of remedies must be express, is to provide, in effect, that the most questionable of private rights will also be the most expansively remediable. As the United States puts it, "[w]hatever the merits of 'implying' rights of action may be, there is no justification for treating [congressional] silence as the equivalent of the broadest imaginable grant of remedial authority." Brief for United States as *Amicus Curiae* 12-13.

I nonetheless agree with the Court's disposition of this case. Because of legislation enacted subsequent to *Cannon*, it is too late in the day to address whether a judicially implied exclusion of damages under Title IX would be appropriate. The Civil Rights Remedies Equalization Amendment of 1986, 42 U.S.C. §2000d-7(a)(2), must be read, in my view, not only "as a validation of *Cannon's* holding," *ante*, at 11, but also as an implicit acknowledgment that damages are available. See 42 U.S.C. §2000d-7(a)(1) (withdrawing the States' Eleventh Amendment immunity); §2000d-7(a)(2) (providing that, in suits against States, "remedies (including remedies both at law and in equity) are available for [violations of Title IX] to the same extent as such remedies are available for such a violation in the suit against any public or private entity other than a State"). I therefore concur in the judgment.

FOOTNOTES

[1] This statute provides in pertinent part that "No person in the United States shall, on the basis of sex, be excluded from participation in, be denied the benefits of, or be subjected to discrimination under any education program or activity receiving Federal financial assistance." 20 U.S.C. §1681(a).

[2] This exhibit is the report of the United States Department of Education's Office of Civil Rights based on that office's investigation of this case. Franklin incorporated this exhibit into her amended complaint.

[3] Prior to bringing this lawsuit, Franklin filed a complaint with the Office of Civil Rights of the United States Department of Education (OCR) in August 1988. After investigating these charges for several months, OCR concluded that the school district had violated Franklin's rights by subjecting her to physical and verbal sexual harassment and by interfering with her right to complain about conduct proscribed by Title IX. OCR determined, however, that because of the resignations of Hill and respondent William Prescott and the implementation of a school grievance procedure, the district had come into compliance with Title IX. It then terminated its investigation. First Amended Complaint, Exh. A, pp. 7-9.

[4] The court also rejected an argument by Franklin that the terms of outright prohibition of Title VII, 42 U.S.C. 2000e to §2000e-17, apply by analogy to Title IX's antidiscrimination provision, and that the remedies available under the two statutes should also be the same. *Franklin,* 911 F. 2d, at 622. Because Franklin does not pursue this contention here, we need not address whether it has merit.

[5] Judge Johnson concurred specially, writing that the result was controlled by *Drayden v. Needville Independent School Dist.,* 642 F. 2d 129 (CA5 1981), and that there was no need to address whether Title VII analysis should apply to an action under Titles VI or IX. See *Franklin, supra,* at 622-623 (Johnson, J., concurring specially).

[6] Cases cited by respondents and the United States since *Davis* are inapposite, either because they involved holdings that plaintiffs had no right of action, see e.g., *Virginia Bankshares, Inc. v. Sandburg,* 501 U.S. ___ 199? *Karahzian v. National Federation of Fed. Employees, Local 1263,* 489 U.S. 527 (1989); *Thompson v. Thompson,* 484 U.S. 174 (1988); *Texas Industries, Inc. v. Radcliff Materials, Inc.,* 451 U.S. 630 (1981); *California v. Sierra Club,* 451 U.S. 77 (1981); *Touche Ross & Co. v. Redington,* 442 U.S. 560 (1979); *Securities Investor Protection Corp. v. Barbour,* 421 U.S. 412 (1975); or because the Court rejected a claim for damages under a statute that expressly enumerated the remedies available to plaintiffs. *Massachusetts Mut. Life Ins. Co. v. Russell,* 473 U.S. 134 (1985).

[7] *J.I. Case Co. v. Borak,* 377 U.S. 426 (1964); *Wyandotte Transp. Co. v. United States,* 389 U.S. 191 (1967); *Jones v. Alfred H. Mayer Co.,* 392 U.S. 409 (1968); *Allen v. State Bd. of Elections,* 393 U.S. 544 (1969); *Sullivan v. Little Hunting Park, Inc.,* 396 U.S. 229 (1969); and *Superintendent of Ins. of New York v. Bankers Life & Casualty Co.,* 404 U.S. 6 (1971).

[8] Franklin argues that, in any event, Title IX should not be viewed solely as having been enacted under Congress' Spending Clause powers and that it also rests on powers derived from §5 of the Fourteenth Amendment. See Brief for Petitioner 19, n. 10. Because we conclude that a money damages remedy is available under Title IX for an intentional violation irrespective of the constitutional source of Congress' power to enact the statute, we need not decide which power Congress utilized in enacting Title IX.

Harassment in the Halls

by Adrian Nicole LeBlanc

Seventeen magazine, September 1993

It can happen at any school, at any time, even among classmates. It's nothing new, though you may not have known what to call it—or what's so wrong with it. It's probably happened to you.

"You're such a nice girl," a senior guy told Katy Lyle, who was a sophomore at the time. "Do you know what's written about you on the bathroom wall?" Her heart sank. And with that, a sadness fell over Katy that wouldn't lift. She had loved school until then, but that moment she began to hate it.

Morning meant struggle. Her mother called into her bedroom, and Katy never wanted to go to school. "I just thought Katy became a grumpy kid," says her brother, Jay, "but Katy was terrified to go to school. She cried every day. I should have figured there was something wrong there, but I was busy with my own life." Katy especially didn't want to take the bus. The phone rang constantly. When one of the Lyles answered, the caller would hang up.

Katie Lyle is a slut, written on the walls of the second-floor boys' bathroom at Duluth Central High. *Katie Lyle sucked my d—— after she sucked my dog's d——. Here's Katie Lyle's number.* It was two walls covered with obscenities about her. The guys called it "the Katy stall." "I was really shocked when I found out," Katy says. "It felt like a big knife. I felt totally stepped on. I felt violated almost—that people were writing these things and thinking these things about me, really gross things." That next week, she told the principal. According to Katy, although he said they would take care of it, he looked her up and down as if she had done something to deserve the graffiti. Had she? What would you have to do to deserve the feeling that the words had made? The closest she'd ever come to having a boyfriend had been the year before, in ninth grade. They only really spent time together on the phone. She considered herself a band nerd. Could she have done something that she wasn't supposed to? She knew it wasn't anything physical, but could she have forgotten something? It was the beginning of a lot more worrying and feeling bad.

Oh, Katy, do me, was the morning greeting. *Are you as good as everyone says?* was for the bus ride home. The Lyles lived way out from town, and Katy would laugh it off for the hour and fifteen minutes the bus ride took, but it would burst out in sobs by the time she made it to the kitchen door. She brought a bottle of Scrubbing Bubbles to school but never used it. ("You could get in trouble if you went into the boys' bathroom," Katy says.) *Katie Lyle gives good head.* They didn't even spell her name right.

Central High School, in Duluth, Minnesota, isn't a run-down, graffiti-strewn school. It's a modern, orderly place. Katy didn't want to tell her parents about the graffiti, but when the school didn't do anything, she finally did. "It's a really gross, weird thing to happen to your daughter," Katy says. "I didn't want them to be disappointed in me." Carol Lyle, Katy's mother, called the school right away. More than fifteen complaints and eighteen months later, the graffiti was still there, hatefulness expanding.

Elizabeth Storaasli, an attorney for the Duluth school district, says that "graffiti was considered a building maintenance problem at the time. It wasn't looked at as sexual harassment." The school claims that it removed graffiti regularly and that the graffiti about Katy would always reappear. Graffiti was just one of those awful things that happened to someone, and this time that someone was Katy. To Katy, it was the worst two years of her life. Gini Stromquist, Katy's best friend, noticed that

Katy went from being outgoing to withdrawn. She'd only hang out with Gini alone: Whenever Gini asked her to do something with a group, Katy would say she couldn't, because everyone thought she was a slut. Gini told her to forget about it, but how could Katy forget? *What are you going to do it with this weekend, Katy?* She wondered which boys had read the walls, what they thought of when they saw her. What did people think of when they heard her name?

Jay Lyle came home from college that spring and decided he couldn't take much more of seeing his sister miserable and his parents embattled, so he took a bucket and some cleaning fluid and went to the school to clean the graffiti off himself. "It wasn't hard—you have this special solvent, called vandal remover, and you wipe it off," says Jay. "I was a janitor at college to pay my way through at the time." He was able to get rid of the writing, but not what was scratched in. That stayed. Around then, toward the end of Katy's junior year, her dad came home from work one day with a name for what was happening to Katy: He called it sexual harassment. A woman in his office who dealt with equity issues suggested that the Lyles call an outside person for help. Right after school got out, Katy spoke to a women from a Duluth group called Program for Aid to Victims of Sexual Assault. "This *is* sexual harassment," Susan Askelin, the former executive director of the program, told Katy over the phone. "It can be as emotionally damaging as physical assault. And you don't have to put up with it." With these new words, Katy's hurt lifted. Then the anger came crashing down. The anger was a much better brand of hurt.

"After she talked to them, she was much more optimistic," her friend Gini says. Katy started dating. Askelin, working as an advocate for Katy, phoned the school to let them know that their neglect of the situation was disturbing Katy and that it actually violated a law—Title IX, which prohibits sex discrimination in schools. When yet another promise to remove the remaining graffiti was broken, Carol Lyle filed a complaint with the Minnesota Department of Human Rights in August. Katy had never told her mother what the graffiti said: Carol learned about it when they filled in the form. "I really almost died," Katy's mother says. "It was far worse than anything I'd ever imagined. We were both in tears." A month and a half later, in October, ostensibly prompted by the formal complaint, the walls were painted and the graffiti finally came down.

People tend to look to the person being harassed for an explanation. They'll say, "Lighten up" or "Blow it off" or, as in many rape cases, suspect that the cause hides in the way the victim looks or in something she's done or said. "When people ask me if Katy knew who did it, it makes me mad," Jay says. "It doesn't matter who did it—although it would be nice to know. What matters is that the school allowed a place in Duluth Central High School that made my sister feel awful. It's as if they said, 'Welcome to Duluth Central, boys. The second stall of the second-floor bathroom is a place where you can write whatever you want and we won't remove it.' "

Blaming the victim makes being bullied seem like something our gestures can control. The blame feeds a fiction: *If I behave well—if I stay a good girl—I won't be harassed.* It's just not true. Anyone can be verbally or physically assaulted on the basis of their sex or sexual identity—boys included. Anyone can be made to feel ugly, exposed, humiliated, and really bad. The weight of the pain can show up in all kinds of ways. "Katy became a hypochondriac," says Gini. "She'd always say, 'My stomach is hurting' or 'I have an appointment with the doctor.' She changed so much that I thought the complaints about the graffiti were just another thing she was complaining about. I never connected her not wanting to be in school to the vandalism. I just didn't think." The weight of the pain can break you, too.

"Faggot," "queer," girl to guy, guy to guy. "I want to bang you," said every morning, freshman guy to sophomore girl. Or he spreads his legs wide open in class when you walk in. Snaps your bra strap. So you stop talking, start sitting in the back. You may even forget what made you want to hide in the first place. Contempt and ignorance taken out on you, now it's taken in.

Rude comments about your period, your thighs, your underarms, your intelligence, the way you walk, the way you smell, the way your voice dips, what you did or did not do with someone Saturday night, the fact that there's no one at all. It can be when a group of people rate guys or girls when they walk by or rate their features in study hall. Or pushing and shoving or cornering you or pinching. The presence of harassment changes your way of being in the world, the way you do things, where you get to do them, and what you'd like to do. It may change your schedule—you switch a class or even a major to avoid it. Your options shrink—you don't feel like playing soccer because of what the guys yell at the girls on the field. The harassment feeds your self-consciousness; it changes you. "You feel like you're a car," says one seventeen-year-old girl. "It's like we're all cars in a car show."

It's not flirting. Eleanor Linn, associate director of Programs for Educational Opportunity at the University of Michigan, puts it simply: "It helps to describe sexual harassment by what it is not. Sexual harassment is not flirtation. Flirtation feels good, harassment feels bad." It doesn't feel like just a joke, even if the person acts like it's a joke. It's the difference between feeling good and feeling lousy—you can tell by how you feel.

A lot of girls try to deal politely with being harassed—by ignoring the person or laughing or just dismissing it—but it's no time to be considerate. You can't really afford to be nice to someone who's making you feel awful, because it adds to the toll of feeling bad. The best response is to try to deal with it straight on, by saying, "Leave me alone," "Stop talking to me," "You're bothering me," "Get away from me." But let's face it: There's no guarantee at all that the person will stop or even take you seriously when you speak out, if you can muster up the courage to deal with confrontation at all. And until people become more educated about the situation—until they learn this kind of behavior is, in fact, harassment, not just an obnoxious boy thing—you may be the one given a hard time for making an issue of it. Friends will try to tell you to forget it. Guys will call you a bitch. If you try to stand up for someone else who is

being bothered—say, a girl who's always being made fun of because she has large breasts—you'll get called jealous. If you stick up for a guy who is relentlessly abused, being called a wimp or worse, they'll say you're in love. You still have to speak up.

If you're being harassed, write about it to document it—just in case other ways of making it stop don't work. Write down the times and places where nasty comments are made or when you're pushed around or hassled. If you want to try dealing with it yourself, the next step is to confront the harasser and tell him (or her) that what's going on is bothering you. You can even write a letter to the harasser describing the bad behavior and saying that you want it to stop. Keep a copy for yourself, and show it to someone else before you send it. If the harassment continues, or if you *ever* feel physically threatened, report it to someone in authority at school. Document that, too, in case nothing happens. Keep reporting it until you get results. Keep track of your own feelings, too. What does it feel like to be treated like this? Did you ever wonder why even the slobbiest-looking guy feels free to comment on how any girl looks? Or why guys' reputations get stronger when they have sex and girls get called sluts? Why is there a word like slut at all?

Your school is responsible for taking charge of the problem and for protecting you from harassment while you're there. Unfortunately, many school officials and administrators haven't been educated about sexual harassment yet. They tend to see the behavior as just "adolescence" or "flirting" or "boys just being boys." But it's a serious thing—and it's illegal. The school is supposed to create and maintain an atmosphere that is not intimidating, hostile or offensive—a place where you can work and learn. A few pioneering schools, such as Minuteman Tech High School, in Lexington, Massachusetts, have workshops to talk about these issues and designated counselors and teachers who help students deal with problems privately (it's bad enough that it's going on; there's no need for everyone in the school to know that you're trying to work it out). Katy Lyle's complaint was settled before it went to court. A Georgia case involving Christine Franklin, a student who was sexually harassed and raped by a teacher on school grounds, went all the way to the Supreme Court and led to a ruling that makes it possible for victims nationwide to collect monetary damages. The result of this is that schools are slowly beginning to pay attention, in part because they have to: It will cost them if they don't.

While the power of the law is essential, it's a good idea to think of it generally as a last resort in terms of harassment. The most important thing is to take the first step. Sometimes people don't tell anyone about being harassed because they think it's a personal problem or something they provoked. Sometimes people don't have the words to describe what they're going through. Other times people are afraid of what will happen to them if they report harassment. Every state department of education has a sex equity specialist. Your state might also have a women's commission. Just write to us, and we'll send you the information.

If you can speak out—on your own behalf or for a friend or fellow student who's being harmed by an ignorant person or people—believe that it will matter. It will. But heroism often does come with a price. Katy's family lost friends who felt they made too "big a deal" out of the events, who somewhere blame Katy and wonder what she did to provoke it. Katy lost a couple of friends, too. Gini disappointed Katy some: She wasn't all that supportive. Katy also lost a lot of time from her high school years. "She was kind of stunted there for a while," says her mother. And even when Katy had pushed the past behind her and gone on to the University of Minnesota, a fresh line of graffiti greeted her there her sophomore year. This time, though, she knew who did it—it was one of her brother's friends. Jay spoke to him about it. The guy was angry about the $15,000 settlement Katy had gotten from the school district. "My tax money is going for this?" he said to Jay. Jay had heard this comment a lot. He had an answer by heart: "Instead of being angry at Katy, how about getting angry that the school principal, who you pay with your tax dollars, didn't think it was important enough to tell the janitor, who you pay with your tax dollars, to take ten minutes to remove it?"

In any case, the price of speaking out isn't as high, usually, as the price of silence. "Katy had to speak out for herself to help herself," her mother says. Her courage made a difference. As of September 1991, every Minnesota school district had to have a policy on sexual harassment. Imagine if all schools educated themselves. You couldn't get away with yelling "thunder thighs" or "faggot" at a person walking down the hall. You wouldn't have to avoid certain hallways because of "slut patrols." You wouldn't have to have that sick, sinking feeling of standing silently while someone—you or anyone—got torn apart. There would be a way to get help. And you might be able to do something else in school besides steal yourself against assault, like learn.

Both Gini and Katy were in college by the time the settlement was made, and they had lost touch. But the nasty comments about how Katy had only sued for the money reached Gini at Michigan Technological University. They made her furious. She knew Katy well enough to know that it just wasn't true. Her anger enabled her to see the pain of Katy's experience that she couldn't see before. Gini called Katy and said, "I really understand now. I'm so proud of you." "The hope is that someday we can stop the bitter lessons that sexual harassment teaches," says Nan Stein, EdD, of the Center for Research on Women at Wellesley College, the first person to identify and research peer harassment in high schools. "By creating more caring and just schools, we can live out the democracy—girls included."

What's Happening to You?

SEVENTEEN, the NOW Project on Equal Education Rights, and the Wellesley Center for Research on Women want to know what's going on at your school.

1. Did anyone do any of the following to you *when you didn't want them to* in the last school year? (Circle all that apply.)
   (a) touch, pinch, or grab you
   (b) lean over you or corner you
   (c) give you sexual notes or pictures
   (d) make suggestive or sexual gestures, looks, comments, or jokes
   (e) pressure you to do something sexual
   (f) force you to do something sexual
   (g) other_____

2. How often did you feel harassed this last year?
   (a) never
   (b) once or twice all year
   (c) once a month or so
   (d) once a week
   (e) every day

3. What was the most serious thing like this that happened to you last year?
   (a) touching, pinching, or grabbing
   (b) leaning over or cornering
   (c) sexual notes or pictures
   (d) suggestive or sexual gestures, looks, comments, or jokes
   (e) pressure to do something sexual
   (f) being forced to do something sexual
   (g) other_____
   (h) nothing like this has happened to me

4. In the most serious instance, who did the harassing?
   (a) a student or students
   (b) a school administrator
   (c) a teacher or counselor
   (d) other school staff

5. In that instance, was the harasser male or female?

6. Where did that instance happen?
   (a) in a classroom
   (b) in the hall
   (c) in the cafeteria
   (d) in a parking lot or playing field
   (e) at a school activity away from school
   (f) other_____

7. Who else was present?
   (a) no one
   (b) a friend or friends
   (c) a teacher or school administrator
   (d) other_____

8. What did you do or say about it when it was happening? (Circle all that apply.)
   (a) nothing
   (b) walked away
   (c) told harasser to stop
   (d) resisted with physical force
   (e) other_____

9. Who did you tell about it?
   (a) no one
   (b) a friend
   (c) a parent
   (d) a teacher or school administrator
   (e) other_____

10. What, if anything, happened to the harasser?
    (a) nothing
    (b) a reprimand or warning
    (c) suspension
    (d) dismissal or resignation
    (e) other _____

11. What does your school do about harassment?
    (Circle all that apply.)
    (a) enforces a schoolwide policy
    (b) holds workshops or assemblies
    (c) hands out educational material
    (d) trains peer counselors or mediators
    (e) other _____
    (f) nothing, as far as I know

Answer 12 and 13 on a separate sheet.

12. What do you think schools should do to prevent sexual harassment?

13. If you've been sexually harassed at school, how did it make you feel?

General information about last year:
How old were you? _____
What grade were you in? _____
What type of school were you in? public / private parochial / vocational
Was your school coed? All girls? All boys?
Are you male or female?
How would you describe your race?

Please mail you survey by September 30, 1992, to *SEVENTEEN* Survey, Wellesley College, Center for Research on Women, 106 Central Street, Wellesley, MA 02181.

Sexual Harassment in the Boy's Room: One teen's true story

by Katy Lyle

CHOICES, January 1993

Sometimes I have the same dream. I'm running home from town on the road around Schultz Lake. It's dark and I'm scared. Somebody—I don't know who—chases me. I feel him shoot me in the back with a gun—and wake up.

The dream symbolizes my feelings about what happened to me in real life. I'd just started high school, and was really excited. You always hear how it's going to be the best, and I dreamed about dating and proms and homecoming football games.

After two months I noticed the boys in my classes were treating me differently. In the beginning they talked to me like everybody else; now they ignored me. "I must be a nerd," I thought. "It must be a character defect."

One day a senior, Chuck, stopped me in the halls. He was in student council, and very active in school. "You're such a nice girl," he said. "I don't know you very well. Do you know what they're writing about you in the boys bathroom?"

Was he kidding? I didn't really believe him, and I didn't think about it too much. I kind of laughed it off. Up until then I was pretty self-assured, soft-spoken but feisty. I had the normal ups and downs of growing up, but my family lived on a beautiful lake outside Duluth, Minnesota. Friends came over to swim, water-ski, or ice-skate. I had a 4.0 grade average and played piano and saxophone in the school band and jazz ensemble.

To be honest, I thought Chuck was lying: "It can't be true. I'm not the type of girl boys write that stuff about." But two weeks later another guy told me about the graffiti in the middle stall. The nicest stuff said I was a "slut." The worst stuff was obscene. I got pretty ticked off and went right to a guidance counselor, a woman. "Who do you think it could be?" she asked.

ALWAYS UNRESOLVED

I had no idea then, and I never found out who it could be. It will always be unresolved. If I knew who did it I'd sit them down and beat them up. I want to know: Why? Why did you do this to me?

The counselor told me the graffiti would be removed instantly. It wasn't—not for two years.

On the bus after school the boys started teasing me. "Can you come to my house?" they'd say. At first I just laughed. But as soon as I got off the bus I felt completely embarrassed and degraded.

The graffiti got worse, scrawled on the door and both walls, carved with a knife or scratched into paint, or written in permanent ink. It was called the "Katy stall." Most boys in school saw it, and a lot of girls knew about it.

I went to two more guidance counselors and then the principal. He looked at me funny, and his attitude was "where there's smoke there's fire." "Boys will be boys" he told me, and "graffiti is a fact of life." He promised to remove it—and didn't.

At school I tried to maintain the image that everything was fine. But when I got home I cried all the time. "What's wrong?" my mom would ask. "I had a bad day," I'd answer. I didn't want to tell my parents because I was used to solving problems on my own. But my confidence and self-esteem shot down—they were nonexistent. I felt afraid and helpless—I felt "voiceless."

I HATED WAKING UP

To say I dreaded going to school is an understatement. I hated waking up. I didn't want to see anyone. I'd baby-sit every Saturday night and practice music at all hours. I'd play Chopin's "Preludes" because they were so sad. I wanted a boyfriend badly, but didn't think I deserved one.

My only good friend, Gini, said: "Try to ignore it. Just blow it off." "It's not your name up there," I'd say. I was terrorized.

I finally told my parents, who got furious. They called the principal to complain many times, but nothing was ever done. Once after school I went into the stall myself and snapped pictures. It made me sick. After two years the graffiti was still there!

A KIND OF ASSAULT

My dad gave the principal a 24-hour ultimatum, then called a lawyer. I called a program that aided sexual-assault victims. After hearing my story a woman told me: "Katy, what's happening to you is sexual harassment, and this can be as emotionally damaging as physical assault."

Sexual harassment. I'd never used the words before, and they gave me a chill. Now I had a name for the nightmare. For the first time in two years, I didn't feel like a victim. There was something I could do to defend myself. I suddenly felt angry, feisty again. I called the school board and asked for an apology from the principal, as well as a letter explaining sexual harassment to students, and a new policy to teach the issue in local schools. And I filed a complaint with Minnesota's Human Rights Department.

It took time and paper work, but the day came when my parents and I faced the principal and a law judge in a closed meeting. A district attorney presented our case, and after eight hours of negotiation all my demands were met—plus a $15,000 settlement from the school.

TURNING POINT

I thought it was over. But the next morning my story was splashed on page one of the *Duluth News Tribune.* Ever since then I've been interviewed for many articles, and appeared on TV's *Donahue* and *Today.*

At the same time another turning point happened. I started dating Eric. He played on the football and hockey teams, but he wasn't like other guys. He didn't believe the graffiti. Because of him, the last few months of high school were everything I'd once hoped they'd be.

It's easy for me to look back now and analyze what I should have done. I wish it hadn't happened, because I'll never look at the world the same way again. It will always take a while for me to trust someone new. But if my story stops one guy from sexually harassing a girl, or stops a girl who is harassed from blaming herself, and helps her take action, then maybe it will have been worth it.

QUESTIONS AND ANSWERS ABOUT SEXUAL HARASSMENT

WHAT IS SEXUAL HARASSMENT?

It's unwanted sexual attention. A classmate won't let up on a crude joke when a girl asks him to stop, for instance. A boss pesters an employee for a date after she's flatly said no. Other forms of harassment include touching or grabbing, offensive gestures or jokes, lewd letters or graffiti, or pressure for sexual favors. Although boys are sometimes victims of harassment, in most cases, males harass females.

WHY DOES IT HAPPEN?

"Many boys feel they have the 'right' to harass girls as part of traditional male culture," says Nan Stein. She tracks school harassment at Wellesley College's Center for Research on Women. Now society needs to send the message to males that harassment is unacceptable, she says.

"Harassment is one person's way of making another vulnerable," says John Guttman, a University of Washington psychologist. By making someone uncomfortable, the harasser feels more powerful. Obviously, not all harassment is intentional. Especially among teens there's often a fine line between flirting, teasing, and harassment. Some people think their crude behavior is flattering. They're wrong.

WHAT CAN YOU DO IF YOU THINK YOU'RE BEING HARASSED?

Here are some suggestions:

■ Try to ask the person to stop. If you can, tell the person you don't like the treatment. Be firm. You can also write the harasser a letter. Name the specific behavior that offends you, and tell him or her to stop. Have an adult serve as a witness when you give the harasser the letter. "He needs to know you mean business," says Stein.

■ Talk to someone. If harassment continues tell a teacher, parent, boss. Enlist an adult to talk to the harasser if necessary.

■ Report the harassment. Go to a school counselor or principal. If you don't get results, check the phone directory for your state's Department of Education. Each state department has one person, often called a Sex Equity Specialist, to deal with such complaints.

■ If you're harassed on the job, call the Equal Opportunity Employment Hotline (1-800-669-EEOC) for information on reporting harassment. This report is the first step toward legal action.

■ Get a discussion going in your school with students and teachers present. "Teens need to openly debate the subject of harassment," says Stein. "They need to negotiate what is acceptable behavior, and what makes for a good relationship. Sexual harassment isn't a fact of life. And while teens can speak out, it is adults who are responsible for making schools and jobs safe and comfortable environments."

A SEXUAL HARASSMENT QUIZ

Sometimes it's not so easy to define sexual harassment. Think about each of the following four scenes. Is someone being sexually harassed? Why? Why not? Answers appear in the teaching guide.

■ Michelle is on her way to class when Ken and James start whistling at her in the halls. At first she's flattered, but they don't stop. When she ignores them, they pin her against the door, laughing and leaning against her. Michelle feels threatened, scared, and angry.

■ When Sara asks her boss if she can switch shifts after school, he replies, "How about a date in exchange for a new shift?" Sara likes her boss a lot, but is uncomfortable about their age difference. "I don't think so," she says, and he replies, "Okay, okay. I was kidding. You can switch."

■ Craig buses tables in the school cafeteria. Every time he walks by Angela and Kim, two popular older girls, they make suggestive remarks about his body and embarrass him. He knows they're having fun at his expense, and doesn't know how to react to their remarks.

■ Darren is dying to date Joanne, and he can't understand why she keeps turning him down. "Why won't you go out with me?" he demands one day. "I like you Darren," Joanne finally replies. "But as a friend. I don't want to date you." Darren can't believe it. He thinks she's playing hard to get. "I'll just keep after her," he says to himself. "She'll change her mind."

Harassment at School: The Truth is Out

by Adrian Nicole LeBlanc

This is what happens to you at school: You're walking down the hall and a guy comes up behind you and snaps your bra or even gropes your breast; a guy leers at you, grabs his crotch Marky Mark-style, and says "Do me"; a counselor who has gained your trust asks whether you've ever thought about sex with an older man; your name shows up on a list being passed around labeled "Piece of ass for the week"; you are cornered by a guy who whispers obscenely about what he wants to do to you. Some of you report being assaulted or raped.

This is just part of what you told us in response to the survey on sexual harassment in schools (done in conjunction with the NOW Legal Defense and Education Fund and the Wellesley College Center for Research on Women) that appeared in our September 1992 issue with the story "Harassment in the Halls." More than four thousand of you responded and, by doing so, took part in the first national survey ever to ask teenage girls about sexual harassment. Whatever people—teachers, parents, other kids—thought was going on or what it should be called before, the truth is out now: You're being sexually harassed at school, and you want it to stop.

Of those who responded to the survey, 90 percent of you attend public schools, 6 percent go to private schools, and the rest are in parochial or vocational schools. The vast majority of those who reported being harassed (92 percent) are between twelve and sixteen years old.

The forms of harassment you're subjected to are varied. Eighty-nine percent of you say you've received sexual comments, gestures, or looks; 83 percent report being touched, pinched, or grabbed. In 97 percent of the cases, the people harassing you are the guys you go to school with. And nearly 40 percent of you say you're harassed every single day.

"This boy started looking at me, giving me weird looks. Soon he was making fun of me, snapping my bra, calling me a fat horse (when I'm not really fat), pinching me (both on my bottom and on the top), trying to go up my skirt, and the list goes on and on."
– *Anonymous, Ohio*

Sexual harassment is defined as unwanted and unwelcome sexual attention. By federal law (Title IX), you have the right to an education free of sexual harassment, and once you lodge an official complaint, it's up to your school to investigate and take action. No case of student-to-student harassment has yet been tried in federal court, but in state courts victims have successfully sued not only their harassers, but their schools for allowing it to happen.

Does this mean that the problem is being addressed on a day-to-day basis? No. First of all, only 8 percent of you say that your schools have—and enforce—a specific policy against sexual harassment. In those schools, 84 percent of the cases reported to administrators resulted in the harassers being punished in some way. In other schools, *the majority of schools,* on the other hand, 45 percent of you say there was no official reaction *at all* when you reported an incident to a teacher or administrator.

It might make you wonder what your school thinks is going on. "Too often, administrators dismiss it as 'teasing' or 'boys being boys,' " says Nan Stein of the Wellesley College Center for Research on Women. "Young women are resisting—hitting back, telling harassers to stop—but when they go to adults, they are not being believed."

"I've had boys put their hand in my shirt, ask me if I was a virgin, and touch my body. It is humiliating. The

teachers act as if there isn't any problem; they try to ignore it, but you wouldn't believe how often it happens."
— *Anonymous, Kentucky*

"For the past three years in high school I've been sexually harassed by a teacher who is thought very highly of. I've tried to brush it off, but the questions about my sex life and the constant pinching and grabbing have not stopped. I've been afraid to report it because I felt that nothing would come of it. I've felt ashamed and wondered if I'm doing something that suggests to him that I enjoy it, but I know that I'm not.
— *Anonymous, North Carolina*

Obviously, you've owned this information. You have lived with harassment, day in and day out, and you know how horrible it can be. In your letters, many of you say that you feel somehow responsible for the physical and psychological abuse you endure, that you're not sure how to respond when you're harassed, that even if you do speak up, no one will help you. As a result, you get depressed, you don't feel like going to school, and your schoolwork—not to mention your self-esteem—suffers.

Many of you also say that you're sick of being harassed and are ready to fight back. Your number one demand: that schools require education on the subject for students, teachers, and the community. Two: You want swift action taken against harassers, from demanding an apology to warning or reprimanding them to suspending or expelling them from school. Three: You say you're ready to lobby for schools to adopt specific policies against harassment. Four: You want schools to create a supportive environment for victims of harassment—by encouraging students to speak out about it, believing you when you report an incident, establishing peer support groups to discuss harassment, and having counselors available to those who have been harassed. And these are just the top four mentions: There were more than twenty-five other specific suggestions in your letters.

Ultimately, you hope to convince people that something sick and harmful, not funny, is going on.

It's your right to demand that harassment stop, and it's your school's responsibility to see that it does. To find out how to fight harassment in your school, write the NOW Legal Defense and Education Fund, 99 Hudson Street, New York, NY 10013.

"I thought I was the only one who this was happening to. I felt embarrassed and ashamed. Getting up to go to school was painful and agonizing. We have got to take a stand against this!
— *Anonymous, Wisconsin*

WHO... reported being harassed?

Girls 9 to 11 years old:	2%
Girls 12 to 16 years old:	92%
Girls 17 to 19 years old:	6%

... do they say is harassing them?

Fellow students:	96%
(97% male)	
Teachers or counselors:	3%
school staff:	1%

WHEN... does it happen?

Every day:	39%
Once a week:	29%
Once a month:	21%
Once a year:	11%
In the presence of others:	92%
Alone with the harasser:	8%

WHAT... form does the harassment take?

Suggestive gestures, looks, comments:	89%
Touching, pinching, grabbing:	83%
Being leaned over or cornered:	47%
Sexual notes or pictures:	28%
Pressure to do something sexual:	27%
Being forced to do something sexual:	10%

HOW... do you respond?

Tell harasser to stop:	74%
Walk away:	46%
Resist with physical force:	40%
Do nothing:	13%
Tell a friend:	66%
Keep it to yourself:	24%
Tell a parent:	18%
Tell a teacher:	18%
Tell a counselor:	2%

WHERE... does it happen?

In the classroom:	23%
In the hall:	18%
On a parking lot or playing field:	6%
At a school activity away from school:	3%
In the cafeteria:	1%
Multiple locations:	44%

Stop Sexual Harassment in Schools

Opinion USA, *USA Today*, Tuesday, May 18, 1993

Sexual harassment is not just a problem for adults; it occurs in our schools and affects girls as young as age 6. Legislation in Congress has been proposed to address the problem. One writer says adults are, in part, at fault.

STOP SEXUAL HARASSMENT IN SCHOOLS

Researcher Nan Stein says girls' plight is being met by adult silence.

They were "subjected to a pattern of overt sexual hostility accompanied by actual or threatened aggressive physical contact and the repeated use of obscene or foul language, including offensive sexual slurs and epithets and other obscene sex-neutral words of expressions directed at females in a hostile manner."

The Tailhook investigation? A police report about a fraternity party?

No, these words are from an investigation just completed by the U.S. Department of Education into the actions of several male elementary pupils in Eden Prairie, Minn., a nice suburb of Minneapolis where eight girls as young as 6 were repeatedly subjected to "multiple or severe acts" of harassment, including name-calling and unwelcome touching.

And this is not unique to Eden Prairie. Similar behaviors have turned up in official complaints in Petaluma, Calif.; Mason City, Iowa; Woodbridge, Conn.; Sherman, Texas; and Millis, Mass. Others have been gleaned from newspaper accounts or letters I have received from parents in Rockford, Ill.; Seattle, Wash.; Putney, Vt.; and Pine-Richland, Pa.

Eden Prairie turns out not to be an anomaly but rather all too typical.

In 2,002 letters we randomly selected from more than 4,200 responses to a survey published in *Seventeen*, 89% of the girls reported being targets of sexual comments, gestures, or looks; 83% said they'd been touched, pinched, or grabbed. And 39% said they had been harassed at school on a daily basis.

The nearly universal feature of most incidents and complaints of sexual harassment in schools is that they happen in public. Students have a right to expect that if something frightening, unpleasant or illegal is happening at school—especially if it is occurring in public—someone in authority will intervene to stop it.

They also deserve to be believed when they report an incident. Yet sexual harassment seems to proceed without adult intervention.

The silence of adults clearly represents negligence, allowing and encouraging the harassment to continue and putting the school in jeopardy of being sued for damages for violating Title IX, the federal law which prohibits sex discrimination or harassment in educational institutions.

This "evaded curriculum" of the schools teaches young girls and women to suffer harassment and abuse privately. They learn that speaking up will not result in their being heard or believed.

Also as a result of that adult silence, boys in school often receive tacit permission to intimidate, harass or assault girls. Indeed, if school authorities don't intervene and challenge the boys who harass others, the schools may be encouraging a continued pattern of violence in relationships.

The lessons which result from official inaction not only affect the targets of sexual harassment but also bystanders and witnesses. Boys as well as girls become mistrustful of adults who fail to intervene, to provide equal protection and to safeguard the educational environment.

If children see that the adults around them are not intervening to stop harassment from happening in school, it is no wonder that other students, the spectators and bystanders, haven't taken an activist role in standing up to question, object and maybe even intervene to stop sexual harassment among peers.

When kids witness the harassment of others and fail to respond, they absorb a very powerful lesson—that they are incapable of standing up to injustice or acting in solidarity with peers who are being harassed or bullied. Life in school may be rehearsing children to be social spectators.

Today's victory may belong to the young girls of Eden Prairie who have established for all of us that sexual harassment knows no age boundaries. But it is a bittersweet victory. Our bigger challenge is to activate all of those kids who did nothing to stop sexual harassment, whether on the bus, in the hallways or in the classroom.

We can claim "victory" only when sexual harassment becomes unacceptable to everybody.

Nan Stein directs the sexual harassment in schools project at the Wellesley College Center for Research on Women, Wellesley, Mass.

What is Harassment?

Sexual harassment is unwanted and unwelcome sexual behavior which interferes with your right to get an education or to participate in school activities. It may result from words or conduct that offend, stigmatize or demean a student on the basis of sex.

The target of the harassment and the perpetrator do not have to agree about what is happening; sexual harassment is subjective. Nor do you have to get others, whether your peers or school officials, to agree with you. Harassment can be a one-time or multiple occurrence. Some examples:

- Touching, pinching and grabbing body parts.
- Sexual notes or pictures.
- Sexual graffiti.
- Being cornered, forced to kiss someone or coerced to do something sexual.
- Making suggestive or sexual gestures, looks, verbal

comments (including "mooing," "barking" and other noises) or jokes.
- Spreading sexual rumors or making sexual propositions.
- Pulling someone's clothes off.
- Pulling your own clothes off.
- Attempted rape and rape.

Some forms of harassment may also be crimes and should be reported to police or prosecutors.
– *Nan Stein*

If you're harassed...
Nan Stein's tips for students (and their parents) who feel they're the target of sexual harassment:

Tell someone and keep telling until you find someone who believes you. Find supporters and talk with them. The point is to find someone you can trust who will take the kinds of actions you want.

Don't blame yourself. Harassment is unwanted and can make you feel trapped, confused, helpless, embarrassed or scared. You certainly didn't ask for any of those feelings.

Keep a written record of the incidents: what happened, when, where, who else was present and how you reacted. Save any notes or pictures from the harasser.

Find out who at your school is responsible for dealing with complaints about sexual harassment. If you feel uncomfortable talking to the designated people, go to an adult you like and can trust. It's OK to bring a friend or parent with you to that meeting.

Let the harasser know you don't like the behavior or comments. If you feel safe and comfortable doing so, tell the harasser his behavior bothers you and you want him to stop. Or write a letter that describes the behaviors you consider to be harassment, indicating that these bother you and that you want them to stop. Keep a copy. Write a letter with an adult advocate and have the adult hand-deliver the letter to the harasser so the harasser takes this letter seriously.

You have the right to file a complaint with the U.S. Department of Education Office for Civil Rights, with your state's department of education, or to bring a lawsuit under Title IX of the federal education laws.

O.C.R. Urges 'Forceful' Reaction to Harassment of Children

by Mark Walsh

EDUCATION WEEK, May 12, 1993

The U.S. Education Department has found that the Eden Prairie, Minn., school district violated federal anti-discrimination law by failing to respond "forcefully" to charges that students as young as age 6 were being sexually harassed by other students.

The finding by the department's office for civil rights is the first involving peer harassment of students in the early elementary grades, according to Rodger Murphey, a department spokesman.

Experts believe the case could prompt school districts nationwide to re-examine their handling of harassment complaints involving children in that age group.

The civil-rights office found that the district violated Title IX of the Education Amendments of 1972, which bars sexual discrimination in schools receiving federal funds. The office acted in response to a complaint from the mother of a 6-year-old girl who said she repeatedly faced sex-related teasing by boys on her school bus during the 1991-92 school year.

The office's investigation expanded to include alleged incidents of harassment against seven other girls, ranging from 1st grade through middle school. It concluded that although the district had a policy in place to discourage sexual harassment, its officials failed to consider the incidents involving younger children as anything more than a discipline problem.

"The evidence shows that the district knew or should have known of the occurrence of harassment but did not respond forcefully to end it," the O.C.R. said in its April 27 letter of finding against the district.

The district signed a settlement with the O.C.R. in which it did not admit to violating Title IX, but agreed to take steps to beef up its enforcement against sexual harassment. It promised to improve training of its employees to respond to such incidents, said it will investigate allegations more thoroughly, and may assign adult monitors to buses or other settings where harassment takes place.

Although the Education Department is empowered to withhold funds from districts that violate Title IX and other civil-rights laws, it rarely takes that step. The Eden Prairie case is considered closed as long as the district abides by its agreement.

Judy Schell, a district spokeswoman, said officials began taking steps to improve its response to allegations of sexual harassment even before the complaint was filed.

"We were disappointed in the findings, but we have agreed to follow some steps they suggested to us," she said. "There are still questions about [what constitutes] sexual harassment with small kids. The [Education] Department suggests that it can be sexual harassment with any age kid."

OTHER CASES PENDING

In the case of the student whose parents complained to O.C.R., the girl; allegedly was called derogatory "sex related" names and faced lewd jokes by boys on her bus, including some as young as she was. Despite the mother's letters of complaint, the district did not treat the incidents as sexual harassment, the O.C.R. said.

The other girls faced harassment on their buses or in school hallways and on the playground, including being teased about being flat-chested, the office said.

The O.C.R. said that "there is no question that even the youngest girls understood the language and conduct being used were expressions of hostility toward them on the basis of their sex and, as a clear result, were offended and upset.

The Eden Prairie complaint was one of three cases being investigated by O.C.R. involving peer harassment at the elementary or secondary school level, officials said. The other cases involve complaints in Sherman, Tex., and Mason City, Iowa. (See Education Week, Feb. 10, 1993.)

Nan D. Stein, the director of a project on sexual harassment in schools at the Center for Research on Women at Wellesley College, said case findings such as the one at Eden Prairie could have an impact on other school districts. But she called on the O.C.R. to issue better guidance to schools on how they should handle student-to-student harassment.

"Until there are guidelines." she said, "I am not going to have any confidence about what standards [O.C.R. officials] are applying when they go to investigate a complaint."

SEXUAL BULLIES

by Ellen Goodman

In many schools, harassment is now the norm.
BOSTON SUNDAY GLOBE, June 6, 1993

It happens in public, not behind a closed office door. There is no "he said/she said" dispute about the facts. Everybody can see what is going on. Friends, classmates, teachers.

A boy backs a girl up against her junior high locker. Day after day. A high school junior in the hallway grabs a boy's butt. A sophomore in the playground grabs a girl's blouse. An eighth-grade girl gets up to speak in class and the boys begin to "moo" at her. A ninth-grader finds out that her name and her "hot number" are posted in the boys bathroom.

It's all quite normal, or at least it has become the norm. This aberrant behavior is now as much a part of the daily curriculum, the things children learn, as math or social studies. Or their worth in the world.

This is the searing message of another survey that came spilling out of the schoolhouse door last week. This one, commissioned by the American Association of University Women, confirmed the grim fact that four out of five public school students between grades 8 and 11—85 percent of the girls and 76 percent of the boys—have experienced sexual harassment.

That's if sexual harassment means—and it does—"unwanted and unwelcome sexual behavior which interferes with your life." That's if sexual harassment includes—and it does—sexual comments, touching, pinching, grabbing and worse.

The girls in schools are the more frequent targets of the more serious verbal and physical assaults. They suffer more painful repercussions in their lives, their grades, their sense of well-being.

But the notion that "everybody does it" is not far off the mark. If 81 percent of the students in the AAUW survey were targets, here's another figure to remember. Fifty-nine percent—66 percent of the boys and 52 per-

cent of the girls—admitted they had done unto others what was done to them.

In public spaces in public schools, nearly every student is then a target or a perpetrator or a bystander—or all three in turn. The majority have been up close and too personal with sexual harassment. Yet we are still grappling with how it happened and how to change the schoolhouse and hallway.

In Minnesota the agent of change has been a fistful of lawsuits. In California a new law was passed that allows expulsions. Elsewhere schools are looking for a magic bullet, a one-day workshop, a 10-point program.

But cultural change requires more than a crash curriculum; there is no quick fix in the creeping court system. Indeed, Mary Rowe of MIT, who has studied harassment for more than a decade, has learned that the vast majority of students won't bring their stories to any formal grievance procedure, let alone a courtroom. They won't tattle-tale.

For a host of reasons, she and others, like Nan Stein of Wellesley College, have come to believe that the schools need a wider range of choices to fill the space between doing nothing and suing. They need teachers who see and say no to harassment in class.

They need designated adults in schools who can listen and help. They need to help students address each other directly and honestly. Indeed, in one tactic a student is encouraged to write a personal letter to the classmate who hurt her...maybe unwittingly.

A school culture of sexual harassment exists in a wide and troubling social context, but change ultimately rests in the hands of the students themselves. After all, not all boys will be boys. Not all girls follow the leader.

So these days, when Nan Stein goes into a school, she says "I talk a lot about courage." She thinks the role that everybody plays, the bystander, is pivotal. "Kids have to learn to speak out, to make moral judgments. I tell them not to be moral spectators."

Sexual harassment is, as Stein says, an older cousin to bullying. Students who understand the dividing line between teasing and bullying can learn the line between sexual play and harassment. They can draw that line.

The most powerful tool for the everyday, garden-variety misery of name-calling, body-pinching and sexual bullying that turns a school hallway into a gauntlet may not be a lawsuit. It may be one high school senior walking by who says, "Don't do that, it's gross." It may be one group of buddies who don't laugh at the joke.

In our society, the courts are the last-ditch place for resolving conflicts. The schools must become the place for teaching basics. Like respect and courage.

Ellen Goodman is a Globe columnist.

Postscript

In this reprint of *Flirting or Hurting?* (November 1996), we have made a few revisions:

- We have included a caveat or warning about role playing (p. 43). In essence, this revision cautions against allowing students to engage in physical contact, intimidation, or aggression even in the name of achieving more authentic performances.

- The handout called "Sample Letter for Student-to-Student Harassment" (p. 60) has been altered slightly but in a significant way. This technique, which has sometimes been imposed upon students, should be considered an option to be used when appropriate. Moreover, it should never be used if there are allegations of deliberate physical contact or assault. In other words, it should be used only to address verbal or written sexual harassment. To clarify the appropriate use of this letter-writing technique, we have changed some of the wording in the sample letter that "Susan" sends to "Richard."

- In Chapter 5 (Resources), we have updated the list of magazine and newspaper articles on sexual harassment (p. 78).

- And, of course, we corrected some typographical errors.

Please remember that this is a library book,
and that it belongs only temporarily to each
person who uses it. Be considerate. Do
not write in this, or any, library book.

DATE DUE
